BOSTON TERRIER

SMART OWNER'S GUIDE®

By Peggy Swager

FROM THE EDITORS OF DOGFANCY MAGAZINE

Boston Terrier, a Smart Owner's Guide®
part of the Kennel Club Books® Interactive Series®
ISBN: 978-1-593787-87-5 ©2011

Kennel Club Books Inc., 40 Broad St., Freehold, NJ 07728. Printed in China.

photographers include Isabelle Francais/BowTie, Inc.; Tara Darling/BowTie, Inc.; Gina Cioli and Pamela Hunnicutt/BowTie Inc.; Shutterstock.com

For CIP information, see page 176.

If you have brought a Boston Terrier into your home from a responsible breeder or a rescue group—or are planning to do so—congratulations! You have fallen in love with one of the most charming breeds in all of dogdom.

The Boston is one of the few breeds that can lay claim to being an all-American creation. With his lively spirit, square build, short head, and distinctive markings, he is instantly recognized. Since he appears to be decked out in a tuxedo, he's earned the affectionate nickname of "the American Gentleman." Artists are as captivated by the Boston as owners are; his likeness appears on billboards, greeting cards, calendars, and more. Something about that flat face and those big round eyes make this dog irresistible.

Around 1870, in the city of Boston, Massachusetts, Robert C. Hooper acquired an imported dog named Judge from William O'Brien, also of Boston. Judge was the product of a Bulldog/English Terrier cross, weighing about 32 pounds and dark brindle in color with a white stripe up his face and a blocky, square head. He was bred to "Gyp (or Kate)," as her name appears on old pedigrees. She was white, low, and square, weighing about 20 pounds.

Out of this breeding came Wells' Eph, a strongly built, dark brindle dog with even white markings; he was low to the ground like his mother. In time, Eph was bred to Tobin's Kate, a golden brindle of about 20 pounds with a short head and a straight three-quarter tail. These dogs laid the foundation for the breed we know today as the Boston Terrier.

About thirty or so enthusiasts in the Boston area organized the American Bull Terrier Club in 1889 and showed their

The Boston Terrier breed has a proud American heritage behind it.

dogs as Round Heads or Bull Terriers. Not surprisingly, Bull Terrier and Bulldog fanciers objected strenuously to the new club and the fanciers' choice of name, since the new breed was so different from their own. The American Kennel Club (AKC) was equally skeptical. However, the enthusiasm of the Boston Terrier supporters did not wane. In 1891, they formed the Boston Terrier Club of America. Since their dog originated in Boston, the name seemed fitting. They succeeded in convincing the AKC to recognize the breed in 1893.

That's when the real work began, as Boston enthusiasts needed to achieve a more uniform look in their dogs. Their efforts paid off in the establishment of a clean-cut dog with a short head, symmetrical white markings, and a body with the square proportions of a terrier rather than the low-slung appearance of a Bulldog.

The Boston Terrier breed standard calls for a sturdy dog, neither fine-boned nor over-muscled. Weight is divided by classes: under 15 pounds, over 15 but under 20 pounds, and over 20 but not to exceed 25 pounds. Unlike its ancestor, the Bulldog, the Boston is free from wrinkle on the head and muzzle.

This is a compact, square dog with a deep chest and a naturally short tail; in fact, a docked tail is a disqualification. The Boston's coat is short, smooth, and fine, and there are three acceptable colors/patterns listed in the breed standard—brindle, black, and seal—all of which must have white on the muzzle and forechest and a white blaze. Beware of commercial breeders selling "rare" dilute colors, such

as blue-gray, cream, or fawn, at inflated prices. Look for a reputable breeder or rescue group through the Boston Terrier Club of America.

The breed standard describes the Boston as a "most dapper and charming American original." A host of admirers the world over would be quick to agree.

Allan Reznik
Editor-at-Large, DOG FANCY

Y ou'll often see a Boston Terrier strike a pose. He'll stand in a regal manner with his ever-alert upright ears, as if his arrival to a high-society party has just been announced, and he needs to allow a moment for the world to take him in. Dressed formally in his naturally short-haired suit-coat set off by a decorative white blaze on his face and chest, this breed has earned the title of "the American Gentleman." But don't expect his poise to last. Once he's assessed the situation, the same dog who showed his aristocratic side will transform into an affectionate, gushing individual who believes that the entire world is his to love. He has no qualms about getting into everyone's face with his characteristic snorts as he greets friends old and new. He's also known for his clownish, entertaining side. The Boston is one of the original American breeds, with boldness from his Bulldog heritage and with calculating intelligence and classic "it's all about me" attitude from his terrier ancestors.

According to the American Kennel Club (AKC) Boston Terrier breed standard, the acceptable colors for the Boston's smooth-coated formalwear are brindle, seal, and black. The seal color appears black except

Did You Know? **The Boston Terrier is not considered a true terrier.** One difference is that most terriers have their own agendas, but Boston Terriers are more content to adapt to their owners' preferences.

that it has a red cast when viewed in the sun or bright light. Colors not included in the standard include shades of gray, cream, and red. Solid colors also are unacceptable; a Boston must have white markings.

The Boston's coat is always short, smooth, bright, and fine in texture. This coat is a delight for dog owners, because the dog sheds little and merely needs a touch-up with a soft brush to keep him looking sleek. And, being a gentleman (or a lady), the Boston doesn't have much of a doggy odor, necessitating less frequent bathing than many other breeds.

The white markings are not just the formal touch to the Boston's attire—they are a particularly important breed characteristic. The *required* white markings indicated by the AKC standard are a white muzzle band, a white blaze between the eyes, and a white forechest (but no bow tie, as some high-class Boston restaurants might demand from human patrons). The standard also sets forth the following *desired* markings for the Boston Terrier: an even white blaze between the eyes and over the head, a white collar, a white forechest, white on part of the forelegs, and white on the back legs below the hocks. The standard goes on to say that, in the show ring, judges are not to penalize dogs for not possessing the desired markings, and that a Boston with "a preponderance of white on the head or body must possess sufficient merit otherwise to counteract its deficiencies [of excess white]."

The ears on this stylish dog are naturally upright, and the tail is naturally short, not to be docked. The preferred tail does not exceed in length more than one-quarter of the distance from tail set to hock. The Boston's eyes are very round and dark. The head should be square and the mouth even.

You'll see a Boston striding along with grace and power. The breed's gait is sure-footed and straight as his forelegs and hind legs propel him with perfect rhythm. There is not to be any rolling, paddling, or weaving as this dog trots along, nor is the gait to be hackney. After all, Bostons have an eye-catching elegance and don't need to draw attention to themselves by picking up their feet unusually high.

Balance is the key for this breed and is reflected in the head, which is in proportion to the size of the dog. As if tailored, the dog's body is rather short and well knit, the limbs strong and neatly turned, and the tail short—no feature is so prominent that the dog appears badly proportioned. The length of leg must balance with the length of body to give the Boston Terrier its striking square appearance.

Boston Terriers are medium-sized dogs and are not to exceed 25 pounds. Weight in the breed is divided into three categories: under 15 pounds; 15 pounds to under 20 pounds; and 20 pounds up to 25 pounds. The Boston Terrier is a sturdy dog and must not appear to be either spindly or coarse. The bone and muscle must be proportionate while enhancing the dog's weight and structure. Dogs who are blocky or chunky in appearance are faulted. Males and females appear almost the same

Meet other Boston owners just like you. On our Boston Terrier forums, you can chat about your dog and ask other owners for advice about training, health issues, and anything else about your favorite breed. Log onto **DogChannel.com/Club-Boston** for details!

except that some females may show a slight refinement in conformation.

The Boston conveys an impression of determination, strength, and activity. The dog's expression reflects a high degree of intelligence. His disposition and temperament are as impeccable as his formal appearance. Of course, you'd expect a dog who is all dressed up to have manners, but the trademark of the Boston Terrier is his social attitude. Bred as a companion, he long ago gave up any scrappiness toward other dogs that his ancestors may have harbored. Bostons tend to be amiable around all dogs and all people. They fit right into family life, loving everyone from children to grandparents. This social butterfly is very friendly and tends to be gentle, alert, expressive, and polite.

Like the most well-mannered aristocrat, the Boston doesn't bark merely to bark. Bostons tend to bark only when necessary. Although he may announce the arrival of a guest, the dog's duty changes to that of greeter once the visitor steps inside. Your Boston Terrier won't guard you from anyone, but he may keep whoever just arrived busy with affection should you need to slip out the back door.

This sleek, dapper dog never seems to have a hair out of place. With his "in charge" attitude, he acts as if the party is always for him. He is lively, entertaining, and not called a "gentleman" for nothing. Throughout his history, this breed has excelled at many roles from show dog to athlete to mascot to hero to all-around great family dog. His good nature and his reputation as an upstanding citizen have allowed the Boston Terrier to maintain a position within the top twenty most popular breeds for most of his AKC-recognized life.

Most Boston Terriers enjoy the company of canine playmates.

I got my first Boston by accident and fell in love with the breed! Bostons are easygoing and wonderful to live with, and they fit in with my active lifestyle just perfectly. They are ready to go any time I am, yet they are wonderfully willing to curl up on the couch with me at the end of a long day.

—Kelly Misegadis, owner of champion Bostons from Colorado Springs, Colorado

Taking your Boston to a training class helps socialize the dog to both people and other dogs. Take time to check out different classes in your area before you plan to attend with your dog.

GETTING TO KNOW YOU

For a lot of people, the Boston Terrier is the ideal family dog. Most Bostons bubble over with affection. They make great companions for people of any age, and they are notably good with children. However, be aware that any dog needs to be supervised with young children, toddlers, and babies. Many children can be too rough with a dog, which is not always taken well—even if the child is acting unintentionally.

If your family includes other dogs and other pets, Bostons take that in stride. This breed typically does quite well with other dogs and other animals. Simply put, they are sociable! But even dogs with a higher social aptitude need some interaction and exposure when they are young, which is why socialization is key to your young puppy's upbringing. Think of it as sending the dog to finishing school to make sure that his manners are impeccable. To nurture your Boston's naturally friendly character and polish his manners, you need to expose him to a variety of people, other dogs, and experiences when he is a puppy and continue that exposure until he is about a year old. If you intend to keep different kinds of household pets throughout your Boston's life, you'll need to introduce your young Boston to these types of animals under your supervision to ensure that the socializing goes well. After all, you'd hate for your Boston's first meeting with a feline to be

Boston Terriers love their people and enjoy the comforts of home.

If you are going on an outing with your Boston on a hot day, be sure to bring along a lot of water and have a way to get your dog out of the heat. This breed has a low heat tolerance.

a run-in with your neighbor's cat, leaving him scratched and with the wrong impression. On the other hand, you don't want your Boston to show too much of his rambunctious side and hurt a cat unintentionally. A little supervision from the start can help shape the right kind of interactions between your Boston and every person or animal he meets.

Another reason for the social sculpting of your Boston is that even though most Bostons have undeniably outgoing personalities, each dog is unique, meaning that some Bostons can show a bit more of a timid side. Early socialization is beneficial for all dogs and can help build confidence in those few Bostons who harbor uncertainties.

TEMPERAMENT AND TRAINING

Don't let the Boston's black-tie attire deceive you. This is a very agile and athletic breed, and the Boston's enthusiastic attitude and love for doing things with his owners leave him open to trying many different things. Bostons love jogging alongside their owners, they enjoy going on hikes, and they can't resist chasing balls and Frisbees. If you have a bit of a competitive side, you'll find the Boston Terrier a willing and able participant, as this bright, intelligent, quick learner has the potential to succeed in many sports. You will find Bostons in the obedience ring, agility trials, flyball competitions, and even tracking events. A

healthy, sound Boston is an athlete who can hold his head up among the best.

It's not unusual for the Boston to show his softer side in the role of therapy dog. Since most Bostons find meeting and greeting people a great joy, they are well suited to visiting nursing-home residents and hospital patients. You'll also find that many Bostons are quite sensitive to their owners' emotions. If you are upset or having a bad day, don't be surprised to find your Boston going out of his way to crawl into your lap and willingly lick away any tears that might stray down your face. However, keep in mind the down side of a dog who is highly in tune to human emotions. He will react more significantly to anger and may become stressed out if you are constantly in a nervous or anxious state. That kind of stress can create insecurity—or other issues, including housetraining setbacks—in a dog.

Typically, your Boston Terrier will want to greet every person who comes into the house. The Boston's greeting is a bit more personal than the greetings of many other dogs. A Boston doesn't merely come up and sniff or walk in circles while wagging his tail. A Boston wants to get right into the visitor's face and say hello. Bostons possess a real talent when it comes to making people feel welcome. With a sniff and a snort of sheer happiness, the dog seems unable to keep a grin off his face, leaving most people utterly charmed.

There's more than charm, though, behind your Boston's greeting and demeanor. You will find few dogs as affectionate as a Boston Terrier, which creates a different kind of relationship between Bostons and their owners than with many other breeds. Your Boston will usually not be happy with a simple greeting and one or two

Behind those big eyes are an affectionate heart and a clever mind.

pats on the head when you arrive home. Bostons want one-on-one time with their owners. You don't need to be gone long to get an affection-filled "where have you been?" greeting from your Boston. And when you're gone for a long period of time, your Boston will greatly miss you. Although Bostons typically get along well with other dogs in the home, your Boston will find no substitution for your affection. He will want time with you and you alone.

Bostons learn quickly and are eager to please. Even though they are relatively easy to train, training is necessary, as untrained dogs may become unruly and problematic. The correct way to train a Boston Terrier (or any dog for that matter) is with positive reinforcement. Do not punish your Boston for behaviors that you don't want; instead, reward him for behaviors that you do want, thus creating a relationship filled with cooperation from your dog.

Praise is important to your Boston, so don't be surprised to find your dog upset or even crushed by excess scolding. Because of their sensitive nature, Boston Terriers take criticism in the form of reprimands very poorly. Similarly, a choke chain is

[My Boston] Sparky makes me laugh. He's always so funny. I take him a lot for hikes in the mountains, and I let him lead the way. He always seems to be able to figure out good trails and how to get back, but when I try to lead, I always get us lost.
—Ramki Marwah, Boston Terrier owner and avid hiker from Monument, Colorado

a poor choice for training; in addition to being too harsh for the Boston, a choke chain can harm the dog's throat, even with sparing use. Instead, grab a treat or a toy as a reward for a correct response to a cue. Since the Boston Terrier is very intelligent, you'll find that your dog won't need a lot of repetition to learn. If he's done it right once or twice, it's time to quit; otherwise, your Boston will wonder why you keep persisting with a particular command and may begin to worry that you want him to do the task differently.

House-training a Boston Terrier can be a bit more of a challenge than with some other breeds. Bostons tend to be slower to catch on about consistently going outside to do their business. Many Bostons do not have good bladder control as puppies, so a youngster may have to stop to relieve himself frequently. Unfortunately, he may be playing in your living room when this happens. For a young dog with a small bladder and slowly developing bladder control, his body just doesn't give him a lot of warning. Since this issue is more about physical development than a lack of response to your house-training attempts, you'll need to use lots of patience when working to potty-train your Boston.

The breed's athletic talent can get some Bostons into trouble when their energy isn't sufficiently expended. They can jump relatively high for their smaller stature,

and this talent, coupled with inactivity and boredom, could lead to problems. So might the breed's astute intelligence. Bostons are focused and alert. Nothing that happens in the household escapes the Boston's attention, leaving a bored dog to figure out how to entertain himself.

Channeling your Boston's energy in a constructive way often means engaging the dog in both body and mind. But, for the right owner, this can be fun. The Boston is a go-everywhere-with-you kind of dog who likes a range of activities. Whether you like to play with your dog at home, want him to accompany you on walks or jogs, or aspire to pursue training for a competitive dog sport, the Boston Terrier is game.

Many people have made the unfortunate discovery that these dogs can have a dedication to chewing. Some Boston Terrier owners find that they need to work to keep chewing issues under control until their dogs are about three years old. Some individuals can also be a bit nippy. The erratic movements and high-pitched noises that younger children make may overstimulate this play-oriented breed and lead to the dog's nipping at the child, albeit in play.

DEMANDS OF A BRACHYCEPHALIC BREED

The Boston Terrier's trademark short nose can sometime cause problems. The Boston Terrier is a brachycephalic breed. *Brachycephalic* is a term that comes from the Greek words *brachy* ("short") and *cephalic* (referring to the head). The brachycephalic syndrome (referring to the anatomical features found in short-nosed dogs) has health consequences; in any brachycephalic dog, the shorter the nose,

Did You Know?

Boston Terriers are amusing dogs who can play at a moment's notice but can then settle down in their owners' laps when playtime is over.

the more prone to problems the dog is going to be. Varying degrees of obstruction to the dog's airway can cause noisy breathing or can result in something more serious, such as a collapsed larynx. Brachycephalic traits also make a dog more sensitive to heat and vigorous exercise than other dogs.

The nose, sinuses, pharynx, and larynx comprise a dog's upper airway. An elongated, fleshy soft palate and narrowed nostrils are the features most likely to cause problems in a brachycephalic dog; in the Boston, larynx abnormalities, a relatively small trachea, and eversion (turning outward) of the laryngeal membrane sacs are also often seen. Put bluntly, those short noses don't work well for breathing. This can greatly limit the dog's ability to exercise even though he may have the energy to keep going.

More severe brachycephalic Bostons may have episodes with breathing difficulties, triggering a noisy "reverse sneezing" effect. Even with mild cases, the owner must limit the dog's exercise and keep him from situations in which he risks overheating. Stress can also cause an attack. Additionally, if the dog begins to panic during a breathing episode, which does happen, his breathing becomes even more difficult. Breathing problems can require emergency trips to the veterinarian. Some veterinarians recommend surgery to resolve more severe brachycephalic issues; in other cases, a dog may be prescribed steroids to help him through rough times.

HOME REQUIREMENTS

The Boston Terrier is a homebody. Even though he may enjoy romps in the yard, outdoor playtime, and going for walks, he's an indoor dog. Being a brachycephalic breed, the Boston doesn't tolerate heat very well and is known to be prone to heat stroke, and his short coat makes him intolerant of colder temperatures. This is a house pet who must be indoors with air conditioning in the summer months and with heat in the winter months. He should not be left outside unattended.

You'll want to buy a jacket for your Boston so that he can stay warm in the cold weather when he goes outside to do his business. And although he should have his own dog bed, he'll still want to snuggle under the covers with you.

A Community of Love

Like many organizations, MidAmerica Boston Terrier Rescue (MABTR) is successful because of its volunteers. The Boston Terrier touches people's lives and brings people together for the greater good. That is evident in MABTR's Boston transport.

While some areas of the country don't have many adoptable Boston Terriers or Boston rescues, there are several overpopulated states. Getting the dogs to people in states where there are few Bostons can be difficult and expensive and can prevent adoption, but MABTR's founder, Jennifer Misfeldt, has a plan to transport Bostons to good homes inexpensively.

The process begins when a potential adopter finds a candidate online, such as on Petfinder.com or adoptaboston.com. After the adopter fills out an application, the rescue volunteer who is fostering the dog calls the adopter for a phone interview. If both the adopter and the volunteer think that the dog is a good fit, a volunteer in the adopter's area will visit the potential new home.

If the adopter is approved after the home visit, but the ideal dog is being fostered several states away, the MABTR transport system comes into play. The journey may begin with the transport coordinator's trying to find someone who already is going to travel the given route and has room for a four-legged passenger. More often, though, a transport route is put together with the help of a number of volunteers who are willing to travel short distances between the starting and ending points. Transporting is one way to help a rescue group, especially when you do not have money to donate or room in your home to foster.

The Colorado Animal Rescue Express helps arrange safe transportation for domestic animals who are going to approved rescues and adoptive homes. Kansas City, Missouri, is a hub where dogs gather to make their way to Colorado. Donna Ronan of MABTR monitors all transports that come into and go out of Kansas City. Sometimes a dog needs a place to stay for the night, as the next leg of the drive does not leave until the next day. Donna finds a volunteer who can give the dog a warm bed to sleep in and help him get on the road the following morning.

When asked why people rally behind this effort so tirelessly for the well-being of Boston Terriers, Donna said, "Bostons just have a way with people. [People] say that they either grew up with one or know of someone who owned one." These dogs seem to charm people memorably.

The Boston's outgoing personality and clownish nature make him a friendly and fun companion.

BOSTON BASICS

This tuxedoed charmer has brains and a sense of humor.

COUNTRY OF ORIGIN: United States of America

WHAT HIS FRIENDS CALL HIM: American Gentleman, Boston Bull

SIZE: Up to 25 pounds

COAT & COLOR: The coat is short, smooth, bright, and fine. Accepted colors are brindle, seal, and black, all with white markings on the muzzle, as a blaze between the eyes, and on the forechest. White may also appear over the head, as a collar, and on the legs.

PERSONALITY TRAITS: Friendly and lively, the Boston has an excellent disposition and a high degree of intelligence, making the breed incomparable as a companion. Bostons like to please their owners, and they should be socialized early with people of all ages and other dogs and pets.

WITH KIDS: Good with children. Supervision is always recommended with younger children.

WITH OTHER ANIMALS: They generally get along well with dogs and non-canine pets.

ENERGY LEVEL: Moderate

GROOMING NEEDS: Bostons should be brushed and bathed occasionally. They are not heavy shedders.

TRAINABILITY: Bostons are highly intelligent and learn quickly. Training is a must, as an untrained Boston can become nippy and unruly.

LIVING ENVIRONMENT: Bostons can adapt to any size home, but they must be indoor dogs, as they are sensitive to weather extremes.

LIFESPAN: 13 to 15 years

America's Civil War ended in 1865, and many believe that this was the year in which a dog named Judge was imported by Robert C. Hooper of Boston. Some records indicate that the dog was imported five years later, and a few sources suggest that Judge was domestic. One fact that is readily agreed upon, though, is that Judge is the dog credited with founding the Boston Terrier breed. A 32-pound English Bulldog/English White Terrier cross, Judge was dark brindle with a white blaze on his face. He had a blocky head and an almost even mouth. Even as the United States emerged from the war, Boston was commonly believed to be the cultural capital of the country, serving as the ideal place to create an "American Gentleman."

THE BREED'S ANCESTORS

The English White Terrier, now an extinct breed, was cited as half of the cross that created Judge. The English White Terrier was an attempt by a handful of breeders in England to create, in the 1860s, a unique terrier for the show ring from some of the smaller, fox-bolting white terriers of the time. This line of terriers was set apart by its pricked ears. Unfortunately,

it's a Fact

The Boston Terrier should have a square head, a squarely proportioned body when viewed from the side, and an even mouth.

Some Bostons have the attitude that they are big dogs in little bodies, and they may not be afraid to take on dogs twice their size. If this is true of your dog, keep him on a leash to keep him out of harm's way.

The Kennel Club (of England) decided that the English White Terrier didn't have enough unique traits to become a distinct breed, and inbreeding of these dogs had introduced too many genetic problems into the breed; all of these factors contributed to the breed's eventual disappearance. Although the English White Terrier lasted for less than three decades, it made its mark on the purebred dog world through the critical cross to the English Bulldog that led to the foundation stock of what would become the Boston Terrier.

The other half of the cross that created Judge was the English Bulldog. With its origins in the British Isles, the Bulldog was a breed of dog used for the sport of bull-baiting. The original Bulldog had to be very ferocious and so savage and courageous as to be almost insensitive to pain. The breed was also used for a while in England for dog fighting until the sport was outlawed in 1835. The dog-fighting ban effected a change in how Bulldog enthusiasts bred their dogs. Breeders began selecting dogs who didn't have any of the ferocity needed for

Did You Know? **The Boston Terrier's tail is never to be docked** and the ears are never to be cropped.

fighting and instead started working to preserve and accentuate the Bulldog's finer qualities. Within a few generations, the English Bulldog became a quality specimen in both physical traits and personality. Without the original viciousness, this breed became a popular companion. The sound temperament was perpetuated in Judge's descendants as people bred to create the Boston Terrier.

A NEW BREED TAKES SHAPE

Judge was bred to several females. One of the more notable breedings was to an English Bulldog, Burnett's Gyp (or Kate), who was described as weighing 20 pounds, with a blocky head and a strong, low-stationed build. Unfortunately, this cross only produced one puppy, named Wells' Eph. Eph weighed about 28 pounds, and was said to have inherited his father's even mouth. He was dark brindle with a white face and white chest markings. Eph was bred to Tobin's Kate, a 20-pound golden brindle. The offspring of this mating gave rise to the Boston Terriers we know today.

As more offspring were bred, and inbred, breeders outcrossed to terriers if the lineage began to show too many Bulldog traits or outcrossed to Bulldogs if the dogs began to resemble terriers. Early breeders worked to create a unique balance. Later, French Bulldogs were added into the emerging Boston Terrier bloodlines to help decrease the size of the dogs, which soon acquired the name Boston Round Heads.

CONTRIBUTIONS FROM THE COMMON MAN

Although aristocrats originally were involved in owning and breeding the Boston Terrier, and many credit people of

Each Boston Terrier's tail is different. Some tails are short, some longer (normally not longer than 2 inches), some straight, some curved, some almost nonexistent. It's not common for [Bostons] to be born with long tails, and docking the tails is a disqualification as per the official AKC breed standard.

—Melany Anaya, Sierra Gold Boston Terrier Club member from Concord, California

wealth and good standing as the creators of the breed, others say that the Boston was in part shaped by those with less means. The early Bostons were referred to as the "stableman's dogs" or "barber's dogs." The employees of the very wealthy who got together to gossip, drink, and pass the time at the local tavern were said to have borrowed their employers' dogs and bred them with other dogs. Although some of the early Bostons were used in the fighting pits, more care was taken as time went on to select for traits that made good family dogs, resulting in dogs with notable devotion to their masters.

In 1888, some of these dogs were shown in a class for Round-Headed Bull Terriers. Many of the fanciers didn't care for the "round-headed" designation and worked to change the breed's name to American Bull Terrier. An American Bull Terrier breed club was formed, and in 1891, breeders established a stud register of about seventy-five dogs whose ancestry could be traced for three complete generations. However, breeding outside of the foundation stock was still being done

to help shape the balance of the dogs and establish type.

In 1891, when the American Bull Terrier Club in Boston applied for membership with the American Kennel Club (AKC), their application was denied for two reasons: first, the breed's name, which was opposed by both Bull Terrier and Bulldog breeders; and second, the AKC's doubt that the breed was sufficiently established in type. At the suggestion of James Watson, a popular writer of the time, the breed's, and thus the club's, name was changed to reflect the breed's city of origin. After negotiating with the AKC, in 1893 the Boston Terrier was admitted for membership, thus making the Boston the first American Non-Sporting breed to be recognized.

Although in the early years, the Boston's color and markings were not very important, by the 1900s these traits had become a part of the breed standard. Some of the early Bostons, not selectively bred for today's color standards, would display too much white on their bodies. Those forebears are blamed when an occasional excessively white Boston Terrier shows up in a litter.

In the early 1900s, Boston Terriers being shown in the conformation ring weighed around 30 pounds. Since pit fighting, for the most part, was illegal as well as decreasing in popularity, breeders again turned their focus toward breeding for companion dogs. This was a natural

True Tails

A Lifelong Devotee

When Nancy Pappas was ten years old, she got her first Boston Terrier. Now, at the age of eighty, this is the only breed she has and will ever own.

To Nancy, these dogs are the quintessential pets. "They were bred as companions, and that is the role they fill the best." Nancy loves these dogs' intelligence, and she'll tell you that they are easy to train. Her dogs will not merely shake a paw on command—they know how to differentiate between their left paws and their right paws.

While there are very passive Bostons and super-energetic Bostons, most fall somewhere in the middle. Nancy's dogs have a yard to play in, but she also plays tug-of-war with them and tosses balls for them. She notes that they like to do tricks to please people; this desire to please is what sets the Boston apart from the other breeds with *terrier* in their names.

Many people fall in love with the Boston's expressive eyes. Nancy says that you can see the dog's mind working in those eyes. The breed's intelligence coexists with its sense of humor; Bostons like to do funny things and entertain their people.

Each Boston is an individual with a unique character. Nancy tells how Katy, her female, loves to dance on her back legs; however, her male Boston will have nothing to do with that.

You will find that most Bostons want to do everything with their owners. Nancy's dogs love to ride in the car and hang out with her all the time. Nancy has observed something else about these dogs: "All of them are born feeling that they will be sleeping in your bed."

One word of warning about the Boston Terrier: the breed has the potential to endure as a favorite throughout your lifetime. Just ask Nancy. So if you are looking for a good family dog whose strong points include loving his owners and wanting to be loved right back, this is a good companion breed to consider.

next step for the breed, which already had a reputation for devotion to its master and family. However, in the 1920s, breeders began working harder to produce more specific markings and body proportions. By the 1950s, the Boston Terrier was very much like the dog we know today. Although many breeds are defined by both weight and height, the Boston Terrier is defined by weight alone. Weight is divided by classes: less than 15 pounds; from 15 pounds to less than 20 pounds; and from 20 pounds not to exceed 25 pounds.

According to the AKC, Boston Terrier Club of America records show that the breed was ranked either first or second in AKC popularity between 1905 and 1935. The breed also ranked highly through the 1960s. Even today, the breed typically remains in the AKC's top twenty.

DOGS OF A DIFFERENT COLOR

Although the traditional colors for Boston Terriers are seal, black, and brindle, genetics allows opportunities for diversity. Most breeders exclude these colored dogs from breeding programs, but there are some who embrace these exceptions.

Cream and red are the main color variations. Red can be influenced by a diluting gene, creating what is called either lilac or champagne. If the black coat color is influenced by a diluting gene, then the coat is gray and often called blue or steel. Both cream and white dogs are born white. Red, also called

liver, Boston Terriers can often have hazel-colored eyes.

The AKC breed standard excludes these nontraditional colors, and purists of the Boston Terrier breed adamantly oppose the breeding of colored Bostons.

MARKED DIFFERENCES

The term *mismarked* refers to a Boston with markings that stray from the ideal blaze, white forechest, and white on the back feet. Mismarks can happen in Bostons of any coat color. Mismarked dogs may display white in the wrong places, including on an ear or anywhere else that disrupts the symmetry of the pattern. However, mismarks do not disqualify the dog from the show ring; in fact, mismarked dogs have earned championship ribbons in conformation.

Splash refers to excessive white on the dog. Other breeds use the terms *pied* or *piebald*. Splashed dogs were used very early in the Boston's development, but breeders worked to eliminate this trait. Still, dogs with varying degrees of splash can still show up in even the best-bred lines; they are considered throwbacks to the early Bostons from the days before the markings were stabilized.

NOTABLE BOSTONS

Although some dog breeds soar to popularity after they appear in a movie or on television, Boston Terriers earned their popularity on their own merit. These dogs

it's a
Fact

Some Boston Terriers were originally used for dog fighting. Although England outlawed dog fighting in 1835, dog fighting in the United States was outlawed state by state and was not completely banned until 1976.

One should not assume deafness is connected to, or the result of, any specific color or absence of color. The only way to know the quality of a dog's hearing is to have a BAER [brainstem auditory evoked response] test performed.

—Krystin Johansen, Boston owner from Corpus Christi, Texas

Thanks to the devotion of early breeders, fanciers around the world enjoy the company of this "made in America" breed.

won over the American public with their charm and sense of humor. The state of Massachusetts took on the breed as its official state dog in 1979.

Former United States presidents Warren G. Harding and Gerald Ford owned Bostons, as did Helen Keller, whose dog, Phiz, was given to her by Radcliffe classmates. Actresses Joan Rivers, Rose McGowan, and Denise Richards are among the Hollywood set who keep Bostons as companions.

The Boston Terrier is the mascot of Redlands High School in Redlands, California, and a Boston Terrier named Rhett (after *Gone with the Wind*'s Rhett Butler) is the official mascot of the Boston University (BU) Terriers. A human mascot dons the Rhett costume, which stands 6 feet 3 inches tall, to cheer on the Terriers at BU sporting events.

Blitz, a purebred Boston Terrier, is the mascot of the Wofford College Terriers in Spartanburg, South Carolina. The first Blitz was a Boston originally named Ka-Dee, who enthusiastically supported her team from September 2003 to October 2008. Blitz took up her post in front of the Gibbs Stadium student section during every Saturday home football game, and she even traveled with the team for some of the away games. At the end of the 2006 season, the athletic department awarded Blitz a varsity letter. Sadly, she passed away on October 9, 2008, during abdominal surgery.

Blitz II (originally named Ayeryel) filled in for the rest of the 2008 season and was officially made mascot starting with the 2009 season. Wofford also has a human mascot who dons a Boston Terrier costume by the name of Boss.

Some people argue that the character of Toto in *The Wizard of Oz* was originally intended to be played by a Boston Terrier based on the fact that in some of the later books, a Boston is portrayed in the illustrations. Artist Michael Muller used photographs of his Boston Terrier, Mirabelle, as the foundation of his book, *The Adventures of Mirabelle.*

Did You Know?

Only Bostons of the traditionally accepted colors—black, seal, and brindle—can be shown in conformation classes. However, dogs of nontraditional colors can participate in companion and performance events.

A Starring Role

Jona Kalayjian has owned several Boston Terriers over the years, but a little rescue dog named Deegan stole her heart and landed a major movie deal shortly after she got him.

The rags-to-riches story started when Jona rescued Deegan and another Boston Terrier from a bad situation. Wanting to give him a better life, she immediately started training Deegan to do flyball, a competitive sport in which each dog on a relay team leaps for a tennis ball and holds the ball in his mouth as he clears a series of jumps, racing toward the finish line so that the next dog on the team can run the course. He took to it, and the team really had a blast together. It was fast, exciting, and, most of all, fun, something that Deegan had been missing in his life.

DreamWorks and Nickelodeon contacted Jona and asked her to bring one of her Bostons to the studio to represent the breed to the producers, director, and casting directors of the 2009 movie *Hotel for Dogs*. They hadn't yet decided on a breed for the canine role of Georgia, and they wanted to meet several dogs of different breeds. Jona knew nothing about moviemaking, so she loaded up a bag of toys and one of her Bostons, Baby.

Jona recalls, "All of the other breeds sat there, looking prim and proper, but Baby, being a Boston, was a true comedian. She reached into the bag of toys, took one out, ran to a producer, and clowned it up. She was throwing the toy around, and she took it to the producer to throw it for her. Back and forth she went, from the bag of toys to the different studio staff members, really hamming it up. She was doing her typical Boston Terrier 'entertaining the people' routine. The casting directors were looking at the other breeds, too, but they kept coming back to Baby. At one point, Baby got her little grin going—the silly grin with her gums stuck over her teeth that looks so hysterical. And they said, 'That's it! That's the breed we want for the movie.' So that's how the Boston Terrier got the part.

"They had seen photos of Deegan, and he looked more the part than Baby did, so they asked to use him for the role instead of her. I had to think that over for a long time, because by then I was so attached to him, and the role would mean that we would be separated. When I made the decision to let him go and be an actor, one factor in my decision was that I felt it would be a good thing for Boston Terriers on the whole. People would get to see what characters they really are, and the part in the movie really shows off that side of the breed. I put in Deegan's contract that when he's tired of being in show biz, he'll come back home. I adore his trainer and know that Deegan's happy with her. We do have frequent visits, but he loves making movies."

Once you've decided to add a Boston Terrier to your life, your search begins. Depending on how you go about it, you could be on your way to finding the perfect pet or to landing in a situation that you'll live to regret. To give yourself better odds for success, you need to learn how and where to purchase a puppy or acquire an adult dog. You need to know how to determine whether a breeder is responsible and ethical, with the best interests of the breed in mind.

Once you find a reputable puppy source, the next step is to decide which puppy or dog will best fit your personality and lifestyle. You need to think about what you and your new pal will be doing in your life together, because that will also factor into your decision.

EVALUATING BREEDERS

If you've decided that you want a Boston Terrier puppy, it's time to find a good

BAER and CERF tests are done by veterinary specialists. Dr. George Strain of Louisiana State University maintains a list of BAER testing sites on his website (www.lsu.edu/deaf ness/baersite.htm), and the CERF website (www. vmdb.org/cerf.html) has information on veterinary ophthalmologists who are certified to do CERF testing.

it's a Fact

breeder. When searching for a breeder, look locally first. This allows you to personally inspect where your puppy was raised and perhaps even to meet the puppy's parents.

The Boston Terrier Club of America, which dates back to 1891, cites in its code of ethics that it is the breeder's responsibility to breed dogs with the intention of improving the breed and to ensure that any dog bred is in good health and free from disqualifying faults. The code of ethics also states that breeder will refuse stud service to commercial enterprises. In truth, people who follow all of the stipulations for breeding healthy dogs typically find it nearly impossible to make any money in the process.

So why would anyone breed? Reputable breeders are not in it for the money. They are individuals who are dedicated to improving the Boston Terrier and to producing outstanding examples of the breed. These people are the ideal breeders to seek out. They will take the time to answer your questions. They will interview you to find out if you know enough about the breed and if you understand the type of dog you are interested in. These breeders will have done the necessary genetic testing to ensure that their breeding stock is healthy. The basic genetic testing for the breed includes CERF (Canine Eye Registration Foundation) testing for hereditary eye disease and BAER (brainstem auditory evoked response) testing for hearing. Since luxating patellas (dislocating kneecaps) are also common in the breed, the breeder needs to tell you if the problem is seen in his or her line and with what frequency, and if any of the dogs have been tested. Reputable breeders understand that they need to have their breeding stock tested so that they're not perpetuating problems that could have been avoided in their lines and in the breed as a whole.

Expect a good breeder to explain to you the finer points of owning a brachycephalic breed. The breeder should ask you about your ability to meet the dog's needs. In addition to the special care that short-nosed dogs require, Bostons do not do well if left for long periods of time without human

NOTABLE & QUOTABLE

In any circumstance where a dog is not of a color listed on the dog application for registration, the owner may include two photos with the dog registration application, one full profile and one head on. The registration application is submitted through the mail to the address on the dog registration application. Staff will handle how it is then reviewed.

—Mari-Beth O'Neill, Assistant Vice-President, American Kennel Club Special Services

A good breeder's time, care, knowledge, and dedication go into each and every puppy.

attention. You need to be willing to make a time commitment to your Boston Terrier.

Boston Terriers are generally medium-energy-level dogs, but some individuals may have higher exercise demands or be more laid back. A good breeder will know the different tendencies in the puppies in their litters and will be able to guide you toward one whose personality and energy level best matches yours.

A good breeder does a lot of work with his or her puppies. A good breeder will handle and pet the puppies frequently while they're still under their mother's care so that the puppies are accustomed to humans and are comfortable with having their mouths opened, feet touched, and ears played with. The breeder should keep the puppies clean, with trimmed toenails. Some breeders may begin the crate-training process after the puppies are weaned. Although puppies are often ready to give up mother's milk at six weeks of age, they need the emotional benefits of staying with the litter until they are at least eight weeks old. In some states, it is illegal to remove puppies from their litters before eight weeks, but this is not an easy law to enforce.

A good breeder rounds out the puppies' early education by starting to socialize them and build their confidence. A breeder who notices shyer puppies in the litter will often take extra time to work with those individuals. Successfully raising puppies to the point that they're ready to go to new homes takes a lot of time and commitment. Seek out those breeders who are committed to the Boston Terrier and are not afraid of taking on the responsibility.

When looking for a breeder, take a moment to decide what you want to do with your dog. Do you simply want a companion to spend the days with? Do you aspire to compete in the show ring or in events such as obedience or agility? If so, you may want to find a breeder with a successful conformation bloodline or more performance aptitude.

BREEDER QUESTIONS

Here are some basic questions for you to ask the breeder:

1. How long have you been involved with Boston Terriers? Beware of people who are just beginning their breeding programs. Unless they've had experience with other breeds, you may end up a victim of their mistakes and learning curve.

2. What are your breeding goals? The breeder should talk about breeding to the breed standard, producing dogs with good companion qualities, and improving the health of the breed.

3. What do you do with your Boston Terriers? If the breeder says that his or her dogs are just pets, be cautious. You may be dealing with a breeder who isn't taking the care needed in his or her breeding program. Most breeders are actively doing things with their dogs, be it agility, flyball, conformation, or therapy work.

4. What genetic testing have you done, and can you provide me with copies of the papers? If the breeder is not willing to show you copies of the test results, or if the breeder says yes but those copies never materialize, steer clear.

5. How many litters do you raise a year? More than two or three? Beware. With all of the work involved in correctly raising a litter, more than three per year are too many.

INTERNET ACQUISITIONS— PROCEED WITH CAUTION

It should come as no surprise that trying to purchase a dog via the Internet carries a risk. However, more and more people are turning to the Internet to look for dogs. While it is possible to find a

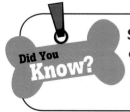
Did You Know?

Some people breed for nontraditional coats; dogs of these colors are known as colored Bostons. Colors include red, gray, and cream. These dogs can typically be registered, but they can't be shown in conformation.

Questions to Expect

Be prepared for the breeder to ask you some questions, too.

1. Have you previously owned a Boston Terrier?

The breeder is trying to gauge how familiar you are with the Boston. If you have never owned one, illustrate your knowledge of the breed by telling the breeder about your research.

2. Do you have children? What are their ages?

Some breeders are wary about selling puppies to families with younger children. This isn't a steadfast rule, and some breeders will insist on meeting the kids to see how they handle puppies. It all depends on the breeder.

3. How long have you wanted a Boston Terrier?

This helps a breeder know if your purchase is an impulse buy or a carefully thought-out decision. Buying on impulse is one of the biggest mistakes owners can make. Be patient.

Join Club Boston to get a complete list of questions a breeder should ask you. Click on "Downloads" at **DogChannel. com/Club-Boston.**

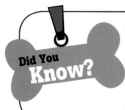
quality Boston online, the Internet also offers more opportunity for dishonest breeders to sell poorly bred dogs. Linda Bollinger and Tia Reinschmidt, both from Colorado, felt that the Internet offered the best way for them to buy their dogs, and they share helpful advice.

Tia turned to the Internet because although she was seeking a dog simply as a companion, she felt that she hadn't found the right one locally. She advises that, when interviewing a seller, you should not tell him or her what you're looking for in a dog; rather, let the seller describe his or her dogs. Tia says that a good breeder who is looking to place a pet-quality dog will always insist on a spay/neuter clause in the sales contract. Tia likes to ask the various breeders what they do with their dogs. All of the same rules apply, just as if you were interviewing the breeders in person. They should live to be with their dogs; not raise dogs to live. And just because they are selling their dogs as pets, this is not a license to produce anything but quality dogs. If sellers can't produce paperwork proving that they've done genetic testing, then they are not sources from which people should be buying puppies. Tia advises you to get the name and phone number of each breeder's veterinarian so you can call and make sure that the breeder has brought the puppies in for the necessary

Puppies get important early socialization through interactions with their littermates.

A Bond with Buddy

"A brave fourteen-year-old neighbor boy rescued Buddy from our house fire when my husband and I were at work," tells Martha Puckett. Martha and her husband had inherited the young Boston from her daughter the week before lightning struck and burned down their home, and she hadn't yet developed a bond with him. She thought, "Oh, the things you end up with from your kids, both the good and the bad." She didn't realize that Buddy would be the good in the bad times ahead.

The morning before the fire, Martha had left Buddy shut in the bathroom with the window cracked and music turned on so he wouldn't get lonely. She and her husband were still figuring out if they could live with the Boston Terrier peacefully. They were also still mourning the loss of a beloved family dog and dealing with the fact that all of their children were grown and had moved out.

Martha got a frantic call at work, informing her that her home was burning down when Canaan, the teenage neighbor, walked by and saw the smoke and heard a dog barking. He squeezed through the window and saved the little guy.

The house was a total loss, and Martha and her husband, Craig, were devastated. They rented a house nearby while their charred home was being rebuilt. "If not for Buddy, I think I would have sat in that dark rental and not done anything except grieve." Buddy's strong spirit and the need to care for him rescued Martha as she worked to rebuild her home and heart. "He offered me the stability I needed and a reason to get up in the morning—to take care of someone. I had to feed him and walk him and do all the little things you have to do with a dog. That's what got me through that time. He has such an unwavering upbeat personality. He loves people and other dogs. He is a great little family dog. He even loved our two cats without a qualm. He is really a no-fuss, no-bother little guy. He just wanted to be with us. He'd lie on the floor of the kitchen when I was cooking and was my shadow around the house."

The couple and Buddy have both been in their rebuilt home now for several years, and Martha says that her daughter has never asked to have Buddy back again, knowing that her mother would say, "Never, ever—he's truly my Buddy!" They have formed a bond that will never be broken.

vaccinations and check-ups. Typically, a good breeder has a veterinarian that he or she has used regularly for several years rather than just calling whoever is available for emergencies.

Linda was looking for a show-quality dog. She worried that pictures she saw on the Internet would not be accurate, so she took additional steps to check out the breeders. She asked for references, and she called those references and asked a lot of questions. She also asked for several pictures of the puppy's parents, as it is hard to determine much about a young puppy's show potential. Linda asked breeders if they had other litters from the same parents and how those puppies turned out. Linda also advises that breeders should interview you as carefully as you interview them.

BREEDING PAPERS

What does it mean if a dog is American Kennel Club-registered? What does AKC registration mean to you as a dog owner? Dogs born to AKC-registered parents are automatically candidates for AKC registration. Health considerations are not a factor. Even if the parents had major health issues, all of their offspring are candidates for registration, making registration alone

no guarantee that the dog is a sound, good-quality animal. The puppy's pedigree will tell you who the pup's parents are and should go back a few generations so you can investigate the lineage. One thing to look at is how much inbreeding has been done, as too much can create health issues in the bloodline. Good breeders will know where health issues have shown up in their lines, and they work to eliminate these problems by excluding certain dogs from their breeding programs and having genetic testing done. Owners of purebreds without registration papers can file for an AKC Purebred Alternative Listing/Indefinite Listing Privilege (PAL/ILP) number, which will allow them to enter AKC companion and performance events.

SELECTING YOUR PUPPY

You've decided that the Boston is the breed for you, you've thought about your expectations for your new dog, and you've done your research and found a responsible breeder. Once you've found a reputable puppy source, it's hard to wait! Unfortunately for prospective owners (but fortunately for the breed!), good breeders often have waiting lists. But waiting for a sound dog with a stable, well-rounded disposition will make the difference between years of happy companionship and years of grief, including health and training issues.

If your breeder is within a reasonable distance from you, and you are able to meet the litter in person, watch the pups and how they interact within the litter. Don't choose a puppy who starts squabbles. If a pup hangs back and seems timid, he will likely need extra effort to build his confidence and work through his shyness.

Look for a puppy who appears healthy and vibrant, taking individual tempera-

JOIN OUR ONLINE Club Boston™

Breeder Q&A

Here are two examples of questions you should ask a breeder:

Q. How often do you have litters available?

A. You want to hear "once or twice a year" or "occasionally" because a breeder who doesn't have litters that often is probably more concerned with the quality of his or her puppies than with making money.

Q. What kinds of health problems do Bostons have?

A. Beware of a breeder who says "none." In Boston Terriers, genetic health problems include various eye diseases, brachycephalic syndrome, and slipped kneecaps (patellar luxation).

Get a complete list of questions to ask a Boston Terrier breeder—and the ideal answers—at Club Boston. Log onto **DogChannel.com/Club-Boston** and click on "Downloads."

ments into consideration. Some puppies may hold back in the company of strangers while other, bolder pups may plunge forward to greet visitors. Take a few moments to study the puppy that interests you. A healthy puppy will explore the world around him, walk with a steady gait, and have both visual and auditory recognition. Unhealthy puppies may appear unsteady on their feet or lethargic. Although it is

A healthy, sound, well-bred Boston puppy will give you years of laughter and loyalty.

strongly encouraged to have a veterinarian conduct a health check as soon as possible after you purchase your puppy, it is best not to acquire a young dog that has obvious problems. Remember, those puppies will be pulling on your heartstrings from the moment you set eyes on them, so use a little tough love on yourself when screening the litter. There is no greater heartbreak than acquiring a dog whose life is cut short due to health issues that were present as a puppy.

If you are choosing your Boston solely as a pet, then championship lineage will not be as significant to you as someone looking for a potential show dog. What will be important is the length of the puppy's nose. Although a very short nose is absolutely adorable, it carries with it more potential for problems with brachycephalic syndrome, which can mean activity restrictions and other special care for the dog and high veterinary bills for you.

A breeder will often allow people to visit the litter and put deposits on the puppies when the pups are only four or five weeks old. However, a good breeder will not compromise on keeping the puppies for at least eight weeks, and remember that some laws prohibit removing puppies from a litter any earlier. Even though a puppy will do fine nutritionally without his mother at six weeks of age, he needs the emotional and social development provided by staying with his mother and littermates for eight to ten weeks.

ADOPTING FROM A RESCUE OR SHELTER

These days, more and more people are adopting dogs. Many people who want purebred dogs turn to breed rescues to find their dream companions. Dogs end up in rescue for many reasons; for example, they are surrendered by their families, they were picked up as strays, they were neglected, or they were slated for euthanasia in a shelter. Rescue organizations vary in how they operate—they may work with one breed only, they may work with certain breeds or types of dogs, or they may work with all dogs, purebred and mixed breed. Some will not accept dogs with certain problems, such aggression issues. Others will not turn away any dog. Rescue dogs are typically "fostered" in the homes of volunteers as they await adoption into forever homes. Rescues are dependent on the generosity of volunteers and outside donors as well as funds raised through fundraising efforts. Some ask for donations from anyone surrendering a dog as well as from adopters. It is important to know how the rescue organization you are considering works before you begin applying for adoption.

Rescue organizations are not the only places from which to adopt dogs. Dogs available for adoption can also be found at humane societies and animal shelters. However, not many Boston Terriers end up at shelters, in part due to the efforts of rescue organizations. Humane societies and shelters often work with area rescues to find homes for some of the dogs they take in and to alert the rescues when dogs of their breed arrive at their facilities.

To understand what a reputable rescue organization comprises, let's take a closer look at MidAmerica Boston Terrier Rescue (see chapter 1). For Jennifer Misfeldt, who has been rescuing Boston Terriers since 2002, saving Bostons has become her life. Running MABTR is a full-time, nonpaying job. Jennifer takes in Bostons of all ages and conditions, and she also accepts Boston Terrier mixes. Unfortunately, she does find herself unable to adopt out all of her rescue dogs; for instance, in cases such as a dog who bites or a dog who is suffering from a terminal illness. All of the rescue dogs are spayed or neutered and receive rabies vaccinations, distemper shots, heartworm testing, deworming, and microchipping before adoption. Not all rescues provide this much medical care.

MABTR works with potential adopters in Nebraska, Colorado, Iowa, Kansas, Minnesota, Missouri, North and South Dakota, Arkansas, Utah, and Wyoming. Like many rescues, MABTR begins its adoption process with an adoption application, which typically takes three days to process. The next step is a phone interview. If all is progressing well, a rescue representative in the potential adopter's area will conduct an in-home inspection. The purpose of the home visit is for the rescue to meet the prospective adopter(s) and to evaluate the appropriateness and safety of the dog's potential new home.

Adoption fees are used to help cover some of the medical and other costs of caring for each dog. MABTR uses foster homes to house the dogs waiting for adoption, and the volunteers in those homes begin basic training with the dogs. Although MABTR's process may seem a bit tedious to some people, be wary of organizations

it's a Fact

The Boston Terrier Club of America or a regional or local breed club is a good resource for finding a breeder or for checking out a breeder you've found online.

that don't take similar care and precautions when adopting out dogs. Less thorough organizations can end up placing dogs in homes that don't suit them or even placing potentially dangerous dogs.

TEMPERAMENT TESTS

Puppies are very cute, but they do grow up—and when they do, we want them to be great dogs. We also want some assurance about a dog's personality when adopting an adult. To that end, canine professionals have devised specific temperament tests to try and identify problems in dogs of all ages. Since temperament is due largely to genetics, but can be influenced and modified by environment and training, temperament tests can give us guidelines, but they can't give us any guarantees.

Here are a few techniques to use when meeting and observing a puppy or adult dog to evaluate the dog's temperament. Clap your hands and observe how the dog reacts. If the dog looks at you and seems comfortable with your approach, this is a good sign. If the dog cowers and shows anxiety at the noise, he may take more time to socialize and build confidence. When making eye contact with either an adult or a puppy, look for a dog who will engage you rather than avoid your gaze. But don't stare with intensity as if you're trying to dominate him; rather, look mildly, with a pleasant expression on your face.

See if the dog responds well to praise. Try playing with the dog and then see if he will follow you. More independent dogs who look for their own entertainment are more difficult to work with than those who enjoy playing with people. See how the puppy responds to petting. Does he try to nip you rather than letting you pet him?

Although these simple checks won't tell you for sure if this is the right or wrong dog for you, they can give an indication of how much work an individual may need. You will have to ask yourself how much work you are willing to do.

Healthy Puppy Signs

Here are a few things you should look for when selecting a puppy from a litter.

1. **NOSE:** It should be slightly moist to the touch, but there shouldn't be excessive discharge. The puppy should not be sneezing or sniffling persistently.

2. **SKIN AND COAT:** Your Boston puppy's coat should be soft and shiny, without flakes or excessive shedding. Watch out for patches of missing hair, redness, bumps, or sores. The pup should have a pleasant smell. Check for parasites, such as fleas or ticks.

3. **BEHAVIOR:** A healthy Boston puppy may be sleepy, but he should not be lethargic. A healthy puppy will be playful at times, not isolated in a corner. You should see occasional bursts of energy and interaction with his littermates. When it's mealtime, a healthy puppy will take an interest in his food.

There are more signs to look for when picking out the perfect Boston puppy for you. Download the list at **DogChannel.com/Club-Boston.**

The nurturing hands of a good breeder work toward the betterment of the Boston Terrier.

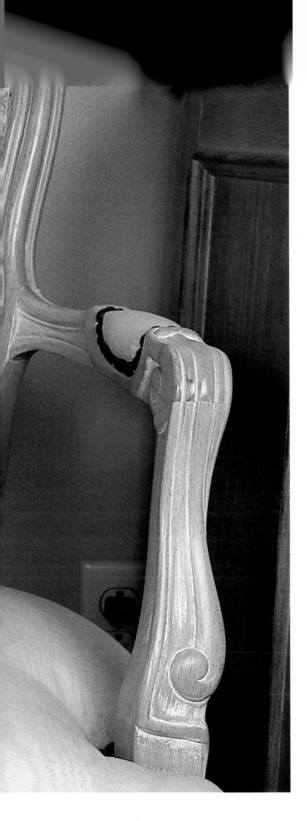

When working to create a safe and comfortable home for your puppy, you need to see the world from a dog's perspective. That means taking a look at things from your dog's height, not just yours. You will need to eliminate hazards both inside your house and outside your house. This often means securing or eliminating many of the same items you would for a toddler as well as allowing your dog to visit only certain safe areas in your home.

You may even need to make a few modifications to your lifestyle, but your dog's safety is well worth the effort. After about a year, most dogs will be more reliable in the house and will require less supervision. However, some Bostons may need you to maintain stricter order and safety precautions throughout their lives. You need to judge your Boston by his individual temperament, behavior, and propensity to get into things he shouldn't. Each Boston is unique.

A PUPPY-PROOF HOME

Your Boston puppy will come to you cute, cuddly, and ready to explore. Puppies are

A rule of thumb when puppy-proofing: if an item is unsafe for a young child, then it's just as unsafe for your dog. Keep all such hazards where the dog can't get to them.

it's a **Fact**

naturallly curious, so you have to take care that your puppy stays safe as he tries to sniff, taste, and otherwise investigate anything within his reach.

Chewable Items

People who talk about their Boston Terriers will often mention that the breed has a reputation for chewing. All dogs are natural chewers as they lose their baby teeth during their first year, but Bostons seem to have a particular fondness for chewing, even as adults. Thus, Boston owners need to be extra-vigilant when it comes to making their homes safe and preventing their puppies from chewing on anything dangerous. Keep in mind that a clutter-free home will be safe for both your puppy and your shoes!

Chewing through electrical cords, for example, can have deadly consequences for a dog. Many office-supply stores sell products to help bind and cover your electrical cords and guard your wires. If your Boston happens to be a more dedicated chewer, you'll need to keep these guards in place even when the dog is an adult.

Look for small items that a dog could choke on. If you have children, small toy parts can pose a hazard to your puppy. A good rule of thumb is if it is not bolted to the floor, then it is free game for a puppy. So look around for things such as socks, coins, or toys. Make sure that everyone in the household picks up after themselves to help keep your dog safe.

Trash Cans

Some dogs become trash-can raiders. While the simplest solution is to make the trash unavailable to your dog, sometimes issues arise. If you find yourself at odds with your Boston Terrier over your trash can, teach him the *leave it* command (see chapter 10) as early as possible. Make *leave it* relevant to your dog's trash-can capers by putting something tasty on top of the can and issuing the verbal cue "Leave it" when the dog goes to take the item. Reward the dog when he looks away, and remove the food item when you are not actively training.

Don't be surprised if it takes the dog a year or longer to become reliable with the *leave it* command. Until your dog learns to leave the garbage alone, buy a trash can with a lid lock or secure your trash can in a cabinet.

Household Chemicals

Some Boston Terriers make great floor cleaners. Any crumb of food that ends up on your floor becomes a treat for your dog. For this reason, it is a good idea to clean your floors with nontoxic cleaning products, as your dog can ingest residue as he licks up tasty morsels. If you have any doubts as to the safety of your cleaning products, you may want to go over the floor with water after using your regular cleaner.

If you have your carpets cleaned, make sure that the cleaning products used are pet friendly. The detergents in carpet-cleaning solutions can irritate your dog's skin, and

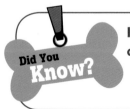

Did You Know? It's a good idea to check your fence for weak spots or small openings through which your dog could escape before you bring him home. Get a lock for your gate and teach your children that they must be diligent about keeping the gate closed.

What your Boston chews on is up to you. If you don't provide him with safe chew toys, you can be sure that he'll find something chewable (but potentially dangerous, such as a stick) on his own.

Don't put a ribbon around a puppy or dog's neck, as he could choke if the ribbon gets caught on a fence or other object.

because the dog sniffs at and lies on the carpets, he can breathe in chemical residue. Long-term exposure to any kinds of chemicals can be detrimental to a dog's health.

Many people readily spray their backyards and gardens for weed and pest control. However, these sprays are fairly toxic, and if your dog lounges and plays outside, that puts him in direct contact with these toxins. Making matters worse is the small size of your Boston Terrier, meaning that pound for pound, he risks more exposure than you do. Other considerations are fertilizers. Some have pesticides in them, while others can cause skin irritations in dogs.

Puppies have to go out to relieve themselves no matter the weather, so consider a doggy sweater to keep your cold-sensitive Boston cozy on potty trips.

Read the package for advice on how long to keep your dog off the grass after fertilizing or look for pet-friendly fertilizers.

All household chemicals should be stored so that your dog can't get to them. Use latches on cabinet doors or store the chemicals in the garage or a secure shed.

Landscaping

Small wood chips or mulch can be choking hazards for dogs, especially those who are dedicated chewers. Cocoa mulch, which is great for plants, is toxic to dogs. If you have a lot of garden space or other landscaped areas, you may need to either create a fenced-off area where your Boston can play or block your dog's access to the gardens with chicken wire or something similar.

Fabric

Some dogs have a habit of licking fabric, such as blankets and upholstery. Fibers from the fabric can be ingested and accumulate in the dog's intestines, causing serious problems. Although fabric-licking can be a difficult habit to break, you can tell the dog that you disapprove of his actions with a quick "No," followed by offering him something safe to chew on.

Toxic Plants

There are quite a few types of outdoor plants, houseplants, bulbs, and shrubs that are poisonous to dogs. Since puppies tend to chew without license, either eliminate these plants from your home and yard or barricade your dog from any possible hazards; the same precautions should be followed with adult dogs who are tenacious chewers. The ASPCA has a poison-control hotline and maintains information on poisonous plants; information on both can be found under the "Pet Care" tab on the

Make sure that your home is safe indoors and out for your curious Boston Terrier.

ASPCA's website (www.aspca.org). There is a charge for calling the hotline. If your dog is in immediate distress, seek the help of your veterinarian right away.

ESTABLISHING BOUNDARIES

Before your puppy or adult dog comes home, spend some time deciding in which rooms of the house he will be permitted. Don't give him full run of the house; setting boundaries for your Boston will make both of your lives easier. Start by creating a safe area in which to confine your dog when you cannot supervise him. Your Boston will not view this confinement as cruel; in fact, he will likely feel more secure than he would if given a large area. Letting a young dog roam freely will make him feel lost and afraid; even an older dog will benefit from the security of a defined space.

In general, the younger the dog, the smaller the area that he will need and want. Limiting your puppy's roaming area not only keeps him safe and feeling secure but also makes it easier for you to teach him the household rules. Use crates, puppy or baby gates, and puppy pens (also called exercise pens or X-pens) to establish where your dog is and is not allowed.

FAMILY INTRODUCTIONS

Everyone will be excited about your new Boston Terrier's homecoming. However, for the sake of the puppy or dog, keep introductions low-key. Your dog needs to feel that your home is a safe place, so don't overwhelm him with enthusiasm. Speak in a soft voice and try to soothe him if he seems insecure. Allow him to investigate, under your supervision, at his own pace. Once the dog settles in and feels comfortable, he will start to act playful and display that natural happy-go-lucky attitude so common to the breed. Let your Boston take his time in getting used to his new surroundings.

If you have small children, talk to them before the puppy comes home about how to play with and handle your new Boston. Use a stuffed toy dog to show them how to hold and pet the puppy and to illustrate the wrong ways to interact with the dog, such as grabbing his leg to stop him from running off. Let them practice with the toy before the puppy arrives home.

When the kids finally get to meet the puppy, have them do so in a calm manner. The kids should be sitting quietly before you bring the puppy to them. Keep in mind that with young children and dogs, you always need to supervise—don't leave them together unattended.

PUPPY'S FIRST NIGHT

Your Boston's first day has been filled with excitement and changes. For puppies, the first night in their new homes is often the first time that they have been separated from their littermates. After the excitement of meeting the family and exploring his new environment, your puppy needs to settle in for the night.

The best place for your puppy to sleep is in a crate. If you can, put the crate near where you sleep. This helps reduce the chances of the puppy's whining and crying at night. However, don't let the puppy

No matter if you acquire a puppy or adult, your new Boston will need your guidance as he settles in to his new home.

You might want to take a few days off to stay home and acclimate your Boston Terrier to his new home, as he will intially require constant attention. If you're there to supervise, you will notice when he needs to relieve himself and be able to prevent accidents from the outset. Even an adult dog will require attention to his potty needs as he's getting used to a new home and new routine.

make noise after you leave, it is okay to let him keep it up for a while before he goes to sleep. Only offer to soothe him during that first night. After that, he needs to accept that crate time means time to settle down, and nighttime means sleeping time.

SHOPPING FOR YOUR BOSTON TERRIER

There are certain things that you need to have on hand before your Boston Terrier's arrival. Pet-supply stores and websites are good sources for finding what you need.

sleep in bed with you. Your dog needs to grow up before you decide if that is going to be one of his privileges. If you don't want the crate in your bedroom at night, select a quiet area in the house for the crate or a room where you can isolate the puppy.

To help the puppy feel less alone, put bedding scraps from his previous home or an item of your clothing (something with your scent on it and that you won't mind throwing away if the puppy soils it) in the crate with him. Keep the new puppy from being disturbed by other household pets or any other commotion. That first night is a great time to begin teaching the pup that nighttime is for sleeping. Puppies who are active during the night are more likely to have accidents in their crates.

If your puppy does fuss in his crate, take him outside and offer him a chance to go to the bathroom. Although he might not really need to go, taking him outside teaches him that fussing in his crate gets him only a potty trip, not playtime or your attention. If he fusses again when you return him to his crate, soothe him for just a moment or two and then leave him. If he continues to

Some ordinary household items make great toys for your Boston—as long you make sure that they are safe. Tennis balls, plastic water bottles, old towels, and more can be transformed into fun with a little creativity. You can find a list of homemade toys at **DogChannel.com/Club-Boston.**

Microchip your dog to guarantee that he can always be identified. Unlike ID tags, which can get lost, microchip identification is permanent. Ask your veterinarian about this procedure.

Dog Bowls

Look for a bowl for your Boston that can hold about a cup of food; stainless steel or ceramic are good choices. Whatever material it is made of, make sure that the bowl is durable. Lightweight plastic bowls can tip over or be chewed too easily. Water dishes can be made of the same material as your food bowl, but should be larger. Some people choose to use a fountain-type bowl, which circulates the water to keep it fresh and has a reservoir to keep the bowl filled.

Crate

You'll find a large variety of crates. Some are made of wire on all sides, while others are plastic or fiberglass with a wire front and vents on the sides. Stay away from crates that have plastic screens or fronts,

Let your puppy explore under your watchful eye.

as the plastic can fall prey to a chewing Boston Terrier.

When selecting your crate, keep in mind that this is going to be your dog's safe place and a house-training aid for you. The right size is important in choosing a crate—it should allow your pup to stand up and lie down with enough room to stretch a bit. A too-small crate forces the dog to sleep in his mess if he were to have an accident in his crate; this is uncomfortable for the dog and will be a setback in your house-training efforts. A crate that's too big isn't good, either. In a large crate, a dog can have an accident and get so far away from it that it doesn't bother him, leading him to think that it's okay to relieve himself in his crate.

Dog Bed

Even if your puppy is too young to sleep overnight in his own personal bed, buying one at the outset is a good idea. Encourage your Boston to nap in his bed when you're nearby to get him used to it. Look for a bed that is easy to wash; there are many attractive and soft styles. Since Bostons are smaller dogs, they don't need large beds, so it will be easy to move the bed around from room to room with you. Having the dog sleep near you will create a stronger bond with him.

Dog Barriers

At one time, confinement devices were limited to baby gates, which some dogs can leap over. Now there are more options, with types of gates made especially for dogs. Some are up to 4 feet tall and include a small interior gate that makes it easy for people to pass through while leaving the dog confined. After you determine which doorways need to be blocked, select

NOTABLE & QUOTABLE

When my dog was two years old, one of her legs would suddenly go stiff or she'd freeze up. The vet said that these were small seizures. One day, I saw that she'd thrown up some tomato plant from my sunroom. She must have had an upset stomach, and with no grass around, she ate some of this toxic plant. I barricaded the plants, and her seizures went away.

—Ken Olson, pet owner from Monument, Colorado

barricades that will safely contain the dog while being convenient for you.

Collars and ID Tags

Collars are great training tools. They come in many materials and sizes, and many are adjustable within a given size range. Leather isn't as easy to clean as nylon, so you may want to wait to get a leather collar until your dog is more mature.

Many pet supply-stores have ID tags that can be personalized with your dog's name and your contact information. Although ID tags have long been popular, and some form of identification for your dog is a good idea, you may want to consider a collar that has the information imprinted directly into it. That way, you don't have to worry about tags becoming detached, getting caught on something, or rubbing against the dog's chest.

Leashes

Bostons don't need very thick or long leashes; a good length for everyday use is 6 feet. You may choose to have more than one leash. Leather and nylon are popular leash materials. Leather leashes look stylish and are quite durable; nylon leashes are easier to clean and come in a variety of colors. As your dog grows and becomes more active on his walks, you may want to purchase a flexible leash that extends and retracts as the dog moves, allowing him to explore something and then return to your side without your having to reel in a long leash.

Toys and Rawhides

Toys are a great way to keep your Boston Terrier occupied and to engage your dog in play. Bostons love it when you play with them. Your Boston Terrier will enjoy appropriately sized nylon and rope toys, sturdy Frisbees, and squeaky toys. A word about squeaky toys: be sure to purchase durable ones that the dog can't quickly chew apart, as there is the risk of his ingesting the squeaking device inside. There are some chew toys that you can fill with treats, such as little bits of kibble. There are others that are marketed as being practically indestructible. Also, keep your dog's toys put away unless it is play-time. This way, your Boston will be more excited about playing with you when you get his toys out, and it also allows you to monitor the condition of his toys.

Rawhides are also used as chew toys, but be cautious. Make sure that they are veterinarian approved, and only offer them under your supervision. As your dog chews on a rawhide, it will get smaller in size; when it gets small enough, the dog may swallow it, presenting a choking hazard. When a rawhide gets too small, take it away and discard it.

Cleaning Supplies

Until your dog is reliably house-trained, you will be cleaning up after him regularly and will need to have cleaning supplies on hand. Because Bostons take awhile to develop sufficient bladder control, put puppy pads on the floor when you're playing with your dog. Some Bostons will suddenly have the urge to urinate in the middle of playtime, so protecting your floors and carpets is the best way to deal with this.

You will need an enzymatic cleaner to clean up any potty accidents indoors. Enzymatic cleaners don't just mask odors, they help digest the organic materials in the carpet to actually eliminate odors. Be sure to also have some old rags handy to help with clean-up.

NOTABLE & QUOTABLE *People often misjudge the magnitude of the Boston's per-sonality because of the smaller stature of the dog. This is a lot of dog! Bostons are cheerfully self-assured, have a lot of personality, and are fairly active. A lot of people don't expect these traits from a dog this small.*

—Nannette Nordenholt, dog trainer from Colorado Springs, Colorado

Some dogs are easier to house-train than others. As a rule of thumb, many Boston Terriers can pose a bit more of a challenge with house-training than some other dogs. Choosing the right technique can help facilitate success. The proper use of crates and confinement during house-training aids the process, while punishment works against your efforts. So gather your patience when working to achieve your goal, and don't set a timetable. Instead, use good techniques, including rewarding the behavior you want, and you will find success more quickly and more easily.

HOUSE-TRAINING IS NATURAL

Like most training, house-training is a process of modifying a behavior that the dog does naturally. House-training a dog is possible because the dog already has the instinct to keep his den or living area clean and free of waste. He doesn't understand that relieving himself outdoors is the best way to do this, though, so that's where house-training comes in. This process involves teaching the dog to expand

SMART TIP!

Feeding your dog on the same schedule each day helps the dog eliminate on a schedule. Setting a schedule gives you a better chance of taking the dog outside at the right times to reward the dog when he goes in the correct place.

the area that he naturally wants to keep clean to include not just his crate or immediate area, but your entire home. By working with your dog, not against him, you can reliably house-train him.

THE WORLD FROM A SMALL PERSPECTIVE

To puppy of just a few months old, the world around him seems huge. In this dog's young mind, keeping his sleeping area clean is pretty much about all that he is mentally able to do. As the puppy gets a little older, his mind allows him to start enlarging the space beyond his immediate sleeping area that he can and will keep clean. How fast that mental development proceeds varies in different dogs and in different breeds. A lot of Boston Terriers seem to have a more difficult time catching on to the concept of keeping their sleeping areas clean, and then keeping entire rooms clean, and finally keeping their entire homes clean. To further complicate matters, Boston Terriers typically take a little longer than average to develop good bladder control, and some may struggle during their entire first year.

When you first bring your Boston pup home, he may need to go out as often as every two hours during the day. You should also take your pup for a potty trip

When you take your Boston outside to potty, let him know that it's a "business trip" if he starts to wander.

We've had dogs that have been in cages in a breeding situation and have never been allowed to go potty outside. Even though these dogs are older, they house-train just fine.

—Donna Ronan, MidAmerica Boston Terrier Rescue volunteer from Kansas City, Missouri

after exercise or playtime, after each meal, and anytime he wakes up, whether in the morning or after naps.

To encourage your Boston to do his business, go outside with the dog on a leash, walk him around until he relieves himself, and then immediately reward him with praise and a tasty treat. By offering him a treat when he does his business outside, you'll find the dog more motivated to cooperate with your house-training efforts. Remember, punishment will only hamper your success.

CRATE-TRAIN YOUR BOSTON

It is far easier to teach a dog where you *want* him to eliminate rather than where you *don't want* him to eliminate. By using a crate or some other kind of confinement, you can work to prevent the dog from relieving himself where he shouldn't, as he will not want to go to the bathroom in his confined area. At the same time, you're taking him outside to do his business so he can learn where you *do want* him to go.

Crate training has other advantages. Many Boston Terriers, especially those

who chew excessively, may need to be kept confined when no one is around to supervise them. In such cases, confining the dog in a crate can literally save the dog's life. Some dogs have chewed through electrical cords and died when left home alone because their owners didn't want to crate them. When the crate is introduced and used properly, the dog will see it as his place of security rather than as a place of confinement—he will readily accept the crate as his own private den where he likes to hang out.

When you crate-train a dog, keep the experience positive. Never use the crate for punishment. Some breeders begin crating their puppies before they go to new homes, which will put you a step ahead of the game. If you are introducing your Boston to a crate for the first time, start by putting him in the crate with something to keep him busy, such as an edible chew or a toy with some peanut butter inside it. Keep the crate near you so that the dog doesn't associate the crate with your leaving. Once the dog is finished with his treat, take him outside for a potty run if he seems restless. If he settles in and decides to take a nap, let him sleep and then take him out when he wakes. Give your dog time to get used to his crate slowly.

Since accidents in the crate are inevitable, be prepared to thoroughly clean up any messes. Don't simply mask odors with vinegar or room deodorizers. Instead, as mentioned, get an enzymatic cleaner,

JOIN OUR ONLINE Club Boston™

How often does a Boston puppy do his business? A lot! Go to **DogChannel.com/Club-Boston** and download the typical peeing and pooping schedule of a puppy. You can also download a chart that you can fill out to track your dog's elimination timetable, which will help you with house-training.

It is important for potty training to be a positive experience for your puppy. Keep in mind that puppies do not develop reliable control over their bladders until they are about five months old. Additionally, dogs are not born with a desire to eliminate outdoors. Dogs must be actively taught through rewards and training that the best place to relieve themselves is outside.

—Lauren Fox, CPDT-KA, director of All Breed Rescue & Training in Colorado Springs, Colorado

which will work to destroy the odor-causing agents so that the dog will not be able to sniff out the spot and want to go there again. Enzymatic cleaners are typically available at your pet-supply shop.

If you adopt an adult Boston from a rescue or shelter, he may or may not be fully house-trained. Dogs of any age can be house-trained, but you will need more patience with a mature dog who hasn't mastered house-training. By following the same steps used for puppies, you can have success with an adult Boston Terrier. Your adult Boston may have been punished for house-training failures in the past, but if you take the dog out often and are sure to reward him with a tasty treat every time he relieves himself outside, you can overcome any negative associations he may have and give him a positive attitude toward proper potty training.

Going outside with the dog on his leash enables you to lead him to an appropriate spot and helps him learn where he is supposed to go, and it will also help you reward the dog more immediately for doing things right. Even if your backyard is fenced, take him out on his leash. Exercise, such as walking, helps stimulate a dog's system to "go," so if you stay outside with him until he does his business, he will start to get the idea of why he's out there.

RECOGNIZING PROBLEMS

Some dogs have issues with relieving themselves in the house that go beyond simple house-training. These issues include marking, frustration elimination, submissive

Your house-training efforts will pay off in a Boston who knows the routine and is clean in the house.

urination, and urination out of excitement, such as when greeting someone. Such issues take specialized training to resolve.

Dogs who mark in the house will typically do so by urinating in small amounts. This unwanted habit isn't a result of the dog not understanding that he should go outside to relieve himself, but a result of the dog wanting to leave scent in specific places or on specific objects. Both males and females will mark, especially if they are intact (not neutered or spayed). Males often lift their legs while females tend to squat to help them aim at a particular spot. If you have an intact dog, spaying or neutering can help diminish marking behavior. Also be sure to clean up any urine right away with an enzymatic cleaner to eliminate the odor and thus deter the dog from using that spot again.

A dog that eliminates right after you leave the house may be suffering from frustration elimination. Crating the dog can often help in this situation, as can basic training to help build the dog's confidence and the bond between the two of you. A clingy dog may benefit from learning the *stay* cue, especially if you teach him to stay for longer periods of time and to maintain that *stay* position when you leave his sight.

A dog who urinates when you approach or stand over him is often urinating submissively. This problem is a result of a breakdown in the relationship between dog and owner. If a meeker dog perceives his owner as too harsh or intimidating, the dog may take up submissive urination, often beginning around six months of age. Resolving the issue means learning how

Don't let your puppy get distracted in the yard. He can play and explore only after taking care of the task at hand.

NOTABLE & QUOTABLE

I've found that house-training is easy if you are consistent. Take them out often, first thing in the morning, and right after they eat. Every time you take them out, praise them. Use the same words every time, such as 'Go potty.'

—*Irene Kruse, Boston owner from Colorado Springs, Colorado*

to not come across as intimidating to your dog, which includes changing to positive training methods if you've been using discipline and reprimands.

Urination while greeting typically occurs when the dog is less than a year old; it can begin as early as four months old. It is usually associated with weak bladder control and happens when the dog is excited. Sometimes this issue is prevalent in certain lines of dogs. By modifying the way you greet your dog, you can help change this behavior. Keep all greetings low-key. When you first get home, use a treat to lure the dog outside in case he urinates. With patience, you can help your dog outgrow this issue by the time he is around a year old.

Three Different Dogs

The Boston Terrier is not the only kind of dog that Kelly Misegadis has owned, but she is loyal to the breed. Kelly had different house-training experiences with each of her three Bostons, and, as a whole, she'd classify the breed as more work to house-train.

She found her first Boston, Hoosier, to be particularly problematic. Even though she'd let him stay outside for a while, he'd always run to the bottom of the stairs and defecate after he came back inside. To break this unwanted habit, she'd put Hoosier on a leash and tie the leash to her belt loop every time he came back inside so she knew right where Hoosier was and what he was up to. If he tried to wander off, she could escort him outside to do his business. Once he finally figured out that he needed to "go" outside, he became very reliable.

Kelly had an easier time with her second Boston, Toby, perhaps in part because after her experience with Hoosier, she didn't have the expectation that she'd be able to train Toby quickly. Toby also would try to sneak off and relieve himself in the house sometimes, but Kelly got right to work.

Kelly feels that male Bostons seem more determined to sneak off and do their business indoors, no matter how long they stay outside. Although she had some adventures house-training Hoosier and Toby, she admits that once the dogs got the hang of going to the bathroom outside, they didn't relapse. To Kelly, it seemed as if a light bulb had suddenly gone off in the dogs' heads, and they realized what they were supposed to do. Now, even if Hoosier gets sick when Kelly is away from home, he will have his accident as close to the door as he can possibly get. Kelly attributes her success with these dogs to keeping things consistent and, of course, positive.

When Kelly got her third Boston Terrier, Elly, a female, she found that two things sped up the house-training process. First, getting Elly in May, when the weather was nice, made the task much easier. Second, Elly learned a lot about house-training from the older Bostons, who were now reliably trained. By watching the other dogs, Elly quickly caught on to the fact that she needed to use the doggy door to go outside.

Kelly found that using a timer helped her house-train her younger dogs. Although puppies may be able to "hold it" for a couple of hours, she finds that taking a puppy outside more frequently helps them learn more quickly. For example, Kelly takes an eight-week-old puppy out every twenty minutes. When the timer goes off, she takes the puppy out and offers him a chance to relieve himself. The timer reminds Kelly to stick to strict twenty-minute intervals. By taking the puppy out often, and encouraging the right behavior, she makes progress more quickly. Kelly cautions that you need never to use any kind of scolding or punishment in house-training, as it is counterproductive.

The health of your dog is a coperative effort between you and your veterinarian. Choosing a good vet and learning how to decide when your Boston needs veterinary assistance will benefit his overall health and well-being.

SELECTING A VETERINARIAN

Every dog owner will find him- or herself searching for a veterinarian at least once. Dogs need good veterinary care. However, not all veterinarians have the same skills and talents or offer the same kind of care for your dog. In addition, some veterinarians specialize in different areas of canine care, such as dermatology, the endocrine system, orthopedic surgery, or ophthalmology. Holistic vets offer alternatives to tradiional medication. There are even a growing number of hospice veterinarians who can help people deal with the final stages of their dogs' lives, ensuring that the time the dogs have left is quality time.

Most people begin by selecting a veterinarian for routine care. The veterinarian's competence and your personal comfort level with him or her are two important

> **Some vaccinations protect dogs from deadly diseases, while others, such as rabies vaccinations, protect both humans and dogs.** A pet owner can contract rabies from his or her dog if the dog gets the disease.

it's a
Fact

factors to consider. A vet's reputation and word of mouth are good indicators of a vet's competence. Ask other dog owners which veterinarians they use and what they like about their vets. Ask if they've run across vets they don't like and why they may caution you against these vets. When calling to check out prospective veterinarians, be sure to ask them about their experience with Boston Terriers. During these interviews, you can get a sense of how well you communicate with each vet. You need to feel at ease talking over issues with your chosen veterinarian.

FIRST VISIT

Whether you are getting a puppy or adopting an adult Boston, you need to schedule a vet visit soon after he comes home. That way, your vet can make sure that your newly acquired dog is healthy. A reputable dog breeder will allow you to have a veterinary exam done as part of the purchase agreement. To some, the idea of returning a puppy to the breeder due to major health

issues discovered at the vet visit seems like guaranteed heartbreak; however, it pales in comparison to the cost and grief that you will experience if your Boston has a health problem that compromises his overall quality of life and lifespan.

Come prepared to your Boston's first veterinary appointment. Bring all available history on your dog, such as his birth date (if known), his vaccination records, and any other paperwork you have. Your vet will want to review the dog's previous vaccinations so he or she can pick up where the breeder or previous veterinarian left off. The vet will record the weight and height of your dog as well as the results of the health exam.

VACCINATIONS

Dogs are typically given a series of vaccinations to protect them from common canine illnesses. Many of them come in combination shots that include vaccines for distemper, hepatitis or adenovirus, parainfluenza, and parvovirus. Some mixtures also include coronavirus. Leptospirosis is another common vaccination, but there is controversy surrounding its efficacy and its potential side effects, which can be dangerous. You will need to consult with your veterinarian as to his or her recommendation.

Adult dogs being vaccinated for the first time or with no proof of prior vaccination will be given two series of shots, separated by a few weeks for most vaccinations.

NOTABLE &
QUOTABLE

Look for signals that you are going to have issues with brachycephalic syndrome. If you notice the dog snoring, blowing bubbles from his nose, or doing more breathing from his mouth than his nose, talk with your vet about the need to restrict activities and to help you determine if nostril surgery is needed to open up the airway, allowing the dog to breathe better.

—Cor VanderWel, DVM, a veterinarian at Fillmore Veterinary Hospital
in Colorado Springs, Colorado

With vaccinations that require two initial shots, the first shot establishes immunity to the disease. The second shot, given a few weeks later, gives that immunity duration. How long that immunity lasts can vary, but most research indicates that vaccinations offer protection for about three years, though yearly booster shots are still common. Some vaccinations, such as those for rabies and kennel cough (*Bordetella*) require only one dose and vary on how long they offer protection to the dog. The kennel cough vaccine is generally thought to be effective for only about six months and comes in intranasal (spray) and injectable varieties. Dogs who are at risk for exposure to kennel cough, such as dogs who are often exposed to other dogs, are advised to get this vaccination; most boarding facilities and doggy day care centers require it. Rabies vaccinations may offer protection for either one or three years, though local and state regulations may require your dog to have an annual rabies shot. Your veterinarian can advise you about appropriate schedules for these and all other shots.

Puppies usually receive their first round of vaccinations between six and eight weeks of age and then get booster shots every three to four weeks until sixteen weeks of age to establish immunity. The extra shot is needed because while puppies are nursing, they receive immunity from their mother, assuming she is vaccinated. When the puppies are weaned, their immunity starts to decline. To establish proper immunity, a vaccination needs to be given after the immunity received from their mother begins to decrease. Since there is no way to tell when that will happen, shots are administered every few weeks to ensure proper immunity.

Rabies vaccinations are typically given to puppies around five months of age. A second vaccine is given a year later; this shot typically provides immunity for three years. Rabies vaccines are regulated by law, and your veterinarian will know how often your dog needs to get booster shots to be in compliance with the regulations in your area.

SPAYING/NEUTERING

Although humane societies and some vets have spayed and neutered dogs as early as two and three months old, most vets prefer to wait until the dog is five or six months of age. Be aware that some females can come into heat as early as six months of age, so be sure to talk with your veterinarian about getting your female spayed at the appropriate time; many advise spaying before her first heat cycle. If your female should come into heat before she is spayed, you will find that most vets are reluctant to perform the procedure until after the heat cycle is over,

NOTABLE & QUOTABLE

Holistic veterinarians offer alternative ways to prevent and treat. One example is acupuncture, which helps relieve arthritis pain in older dogs and can also reduce the need for drugs with undesirable side effects.
—Jim Friedly, DVM, a certified holistic veterinarian at the Natural Health Care Center for Animals in Colorado Springs, Colorado

Just like with infants, puppies need a series of vaccinations to ensure that they stay healthy during their first year of life. Download a vaccination chart from **DogChannel.com/Club-Boston** that you can fill out for your Boston Terrier.

as the surgery is riskier for a dog in heat. You will also find that the three weeks of your dog's heat cycle will seem like a very long time. During that time, you will need to keep her away from any intact males, or she could become pregnant.

The neutering process for a male dog is a relatively easy surgery. Neutering your male helps prevent unwanted behaviors, such as marking, and creates a more content dog who is less likely to want to wander. A neutered male will also be less aggressive than an intact male.

HOLISTIC VETERINARIANS

Holistic veterinarians use alternative modalities such as acupuncture, chiropractic, homeopathy, herbal medicine, and nutritional therapy to treat or prevent health problems in dogs or to complement traditional veterinary treatments. Holistic veterinarians often have in-depth training in canine nutrition, allowing them to resolve many health issues by changing and improving the quality of the diet. As your dog ages, a holistic veterinarian can play an important role in maintaining the quality of your dog's life.

Some holistic veterinarians began as conventional veterinarians. For example, Dr. Jim Friedly was a conventional vet for twenty-five years. Traditional solutions to his own work-related injury left him frustrated, but after an acupuncturist resolved his issue, he decided to go back to school to learn about alternative-medicine techniques for animals. His journey has led him through courses in holistic modalities including acupuncture, animal chiropractic, Chinese and Western herbal remedies, and homeopathy.

Dr. Friedly sees many dogs with pain issues, including arthritis, while skin problems and allergies rank a close second. He has a lot of success in solving chronic gastrointestinal problems, sometimes seen as dogs age. Some of his clients come to him after suffering serious side effects from traditional medicine. For example, managing seizures often becomes a balance between toxicity of the medicine and the severity of the seizures. Friedly has been able to get some dogs off phenobarbital, commonly prescribed as a seizure medication in canines. He also deals with aggression and fearfulness by using a combination of herbal therapy and nutrition.

The American Holistic Veterinary Medical Association maintains a list of its members, along with modalities practiced, on its website (www.ahvma.org). Look for a holistic vet who has had specialized training and at least a few years of experience with patients rather than a traditional veterinarian who dabbles in alternative medicine. Holistic veterinary medicine takes additional training and, for many, it is a lifelong pursuit.

COMMON CANINE HEALTH PROBLEMS

Just like us, dogs can sometimes feel under the weather and suffer from mild illnesses or injuries. Here are some guidelines to help you determine if your dog needs a visit to the veterinarian or just some extra TLC.

Your Boston relies on you to provide him with proper healthcare. Select a knowledgeable and caring veterinarian.

Did You Know?

Canine influenza is a problematic and at times deadly disease that can spread quickly among dogs. A vaccine has been approved for canine influenza; however, the vaccine works to lessen the impact of the disease rather than prevent the disease. More research is underway to find a better solution.

Colds

Dogs don't get colds in the same way that people do, but they can experience similar symptoms. If your puppy does a lot of snorting and sneezing or has bubbling from the nose, you should check with your vet to see if your Boston is experiencing problems due to brachycephalic syndrome. If your dog is coughing, has excess nasal congestion, and is acting listless, you need to seek veterinary attention. A cough or runny nose could mean allergies, and if this is the case, your vet can advise you about how to eliminate triggers that aggravate the situation. For example, if the dog displays allergic symptoms during times of high pollen, you may need to bathe him to remove any allergens in his coat after he's spent time outdoors.

Canine Influenza

In 2004, canine influenza, also known as the "dog flu," was a newly emerging virus found to cause a contagious respiratory infection in any dog, regardless of breed or age. Many dogs exposed to the virus do not develop any clinical signs of illness. Dogs who are ill may at first appear to have kennel cough. However, the cough associated with canine influenza persists much longer, often lasting for ten to twenty-one days.

Affected dogs may also have nasal discharge and low-grade fevers. Canine influenza can progress to pneumonia, in which case the dog may require supportive care and hospitalization. With early veterinary attention, the fatality rate from influenza is very low. There are no known cases of canine influenza infecting humans.

Vomiting and Diarrhea

Sometimes, when a dog eats something that disagrees with his system, he can suffer some kind of gastric upset. You can often help your dog get over this at home with some dietary changes. A bland diet of white rice with a little lean cooked ground beef or chicken can help the dog get back on track. If the dog has a normal energy level and is eating and drinking, you can simply monitor him for couple of days and see if the vomiting or diarrhea stops. However, if the dog becomes listless or refuses to eat, or if the problem does not resolve on its own after two days on the modified diet, seek veterinary help.

Minor Cuts and Scrapes

If your dog has a minor abrasion, wash the area with warm water to which you've added a dash of salt. Dry the area with a clean towel. If the cut is superficial, you can simply keep an eye on it for a few days. If the abrasion is a little deeper, use a topical antibiotic ointment on the area, making sure that it is kept clean. For deep cuts or cuts that become infected, seek the help of a veterinarian.

Anal Glands

Boston Terriers and other smaller dogs tend to have more problems with their anal glands than bigger dogs do. Smaller dogs have smaller channels to drain their

Did You Know?

Although your vet will look into your dog's eyes as part of a routine check-up, only a veterinary ophthalmologist can determine if a dog has any major eye issues, such as cataracts. For these types of problems, a dog needs to be CERF-tested by an approved canine ophthalmologist.

Select a trusted veterinarian to care for your Boston at all stages of your dog's life.

glands, which can result in a build-up of fluid that causes discomfort to the dog. You may notice a problem if you see your dog scooting around on his behind, trying to relieve the pressure. When fluid builds up in the anal glands, you need to have the dog's glands expressed. Your veterinarian, a vet tech, or an experienced groomer can express the glands for you. Your veterinarian can teach you how to express the anal glands, but this can be a messy task that you may not want to attempt. If you are going to express the glands yourself, be sure to get adequate instructions. If you do it incorrectly, you can rupture a gland, which is a very serious situation.

Your dog's scooting around on his rear end frequently could be a sign of allergies instead of anal-sac problems, so have him checked out by your veterinarian.

Sound breeding practices give dogs of any breed a good chance of being healthy. Health-conscious breeders do genetic testing and remove from their breeding programs any individuals with health problems. They also learn to inbreed with caution. Although inbreeding is done to try and preserve desirable traits, too much inbreeding destroys the genetic diversity needed to help maintain good health. Unfortunately, even the best breeding programs can unintentionally produce individuals with health issues specific to the Boston Terrier. There are other problems, such as parasites and allergies, that can affect dogs of any breed, regardless of heredity.

EYE CONDITIONS IN BOSTON TERRIER

The care of your Boston's eyes and vision is important to his overall well-being. Bostons are more susceptible than average to eye problems; a number of hereditary eye diseases are seen in the breed, and the prominence of their eyes predisposes Bostons to certain types of injuries and irritations.

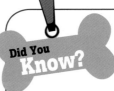

Did You Know?

If your Boston has issues with brachycephalic syndrome that don't require surgery, you may want to skip the steroids and look for alternative ways of managing his health. A holistic vet is often a good resource.

Corneal Ulcers

Corneal ulcers are common in Boston Terriers. These ulcers result from injuries to the eye or from other eye issues that cause irritation. Corneal ulcers can become infected and difficult to treat.

Preventing eye injuries is important. Keep your Boston Terrier away from thorny plants and out of dusty conditions. Also, don't use strong household cleaners. If you can smell the cleaner, then its chemicals can become an eye irritant for your Boston.

Glaucoma

The Boston Terrier is among the many breeds that can be affected by glaucoma. Glaucoma causes a build-up in eye pressure, which eventually results in blindness in most individuals. Canine ophthalmologists can often help preserve eyesight with special medication if the condition is recognized early.

Cataracts

A cataract is a clouding of the eye's lens, which can lead to blindness. Early-onset hereditary cataracts may be visible in Boston Terriers before one year of age, sometimes as early as eight to twelve weeks, while late-onset hereditary cataracts usually do not appear until between four and six years of age. Cataracts can also develop in senior Bostons, and although there is the risk of blindness, the dog's less active state makes it easier for him to tolerate the effects of cataracts. Cataracts can be removed surgically, but the procedure is expensive, often costing several thousand dollars per eye. Annual CERF testing on all potential breeding animals should be considered a requirement for breeders.

Cherry Eye

Cherry eye can resemble a tumor in the eye because it usually looks like a bright red protruding mass. Cherry eye is caused by the tear gland's popping out of its normal position. In the Boston Terrier's eye, there is a third eyelid where this gland is located. If the gland pops out, it swells up outside the eye, causing the unsightly "cherry" eye. This problem must be corrected surgically, but it is a fairly common procedure.

Corneal Dystrophy

Corneal dystrophy usually develops in Boston Terriers between five and seven years of age and appears as opacities in one or both eyes. The opacities can vary in size, shape, and number; often the entire cornea becomes involved. Boston Terriers are prone to corneal endothelial dystrophy, which is a build-up of fluid in inner layer of the cornea. Corneal dystrophy in itself usually does not cause discomfort to an affected dog, but corneal ulcers, which are painful and difficult to treat, can develop as a result of the corneal dystrophy.

Distichiasis

Distichiasis—abnormally placed hairs on the inner surface of the eyelid—is one of the causes of corneal ulcers. Constant irritation from the hairs make it hard for the ulcers to heal. Removal of the hair can often solve this problem.

Entropion

Entropion is also a result of irritation caused by hair. The lower lid margin rolls inward, causing the lashes of the lower lid to rub against the eyeball. The irritation can cause redness, inflammation, infection, or corneal ulcers. Surgery can help solve the problem.

Boston Terriers have fewer major health issues compared to some of the other popular breeds. [There's] occasional eye irritation and snoring, but they don't have a lot of musculoskeletal problems or metabolic issues and often live full and long lives.

—Jim Friedly, DVM, a certified holistic veterinarian at the Natural Health Care Center for Animals in Colorado Springs, Colorado

Keratoconjunctivitis Sicca

Keratoconjunctivitis sicca, also known as *dry eye*, is a result of inadequate tear production. According to BostonTerrierHub.com, it occurs in one out of fifty Boston Terriers. Dry eye develops very early in life and can lead to eye infections. Cyclosporine administered daily in eye-drop form is a common treatment.

DEAFNESS

Although not all deafness is genetic, hereditary deafness can be prevented by eliminating deaf and partially deaf dogs from breeding programs. Dogs who are deaf in one ear can function fine as pets with owners who understand their needs; however, if breeders use these dogs to produce puppies, the offspring can be completely deaf. The only way to verify the hearing status of breeding stock is through brainstem auditory evoked response (BAER) testing, which can identify if a dog can hear in one or both ears as well as the quality of hearing.

BRACHYCEPHALIC SYNDROME

We've already discussed brachycephalic syndrome—respiratory problems due to the structure of the Boston's short muzzle and pushed-in nose. Ironically, one solution to this issue is in the hands of the breeder—the same breeder who works to perpetuate the Boston Terrier's trademark brachycephalic features. There are breeders who are working to breed for less compressed noses; unfortunately, some breeders feel that this can work against them in the show ring.

A dog with brachycephalic syndrome requires owners who will take everyday steps to manage the problem; precautions including limiting exercise and making sure that the dog doesn't overheat. Stress and excitement—even simple things, such as enthusiasm over your coming home—can trigger breathing distress in an affected Boston Terrier.

Trying to find relief for brachycephalic dogs often sends people to their veterinarians. The goal in the treatment of brachycephalic airway problems is to make it easier for the animal to breathe. Surgery often becomes the solution for more severe cases. Steroids, sometimes in combination with an antihistamine, are used for less severe cases but are considered short-term fixes.

For people who want a more holistic approach to resolving milder breathing issues, holistic vet Dr. Martin Goldstein recommends a commercially available natural herb-and-honey cough syrup for humans or an over-the-counter herbal expectorant that contains guaifenesin.

Kelly Misegadis found a unique way to help her Boston Terrier, Hoosier, through his breathing problems. Her veterinarian taught her how to employ a two-pronged approach of getting Hoosier to breathe though his mouth by plugging his nose while soothing him by stroking his neck. Relaxation is key to stopping a dog's problematic breathing episodes, while stress and panic can exacerbate the problem. With this in mind, using what she'd learned

CERF and Your Dog's Eyes

The Canine Eye Registration Foundation (CERF) hosts a centralized national registry with the goal of identifying hereditary eye diseases in purebred dogs. CERF issues clearances to dogs who have tested free of heritable eye diseases and collects data on all dogs who undergo CERF exams. The information in the database is useful for researching trends in eye disease and breed susceptibility. The CERF exam, which is much like a human eye exam in which the eyes need to be dilated, must be done by a CERF-approved veterinary ophthalmologist who is a member of the American College of Veterinary Ophthalmologists. Dogs intended for breeding need to be CERF-tested annually because although some hereditary eye problems are present at birth, others can develop over time.

Some dog owners who never plan on showing or breeding their dogs wonder if pets need to come from CERF-tested parents. Serious eye conditions that are passed along genetically can compromise the quality of pet's life and result in excess expense for the owner. By purchasing a dog from a breeder who is not invested in the total health of his or dogs, including the dog's eye health, you are only perpetuating poor breeding practices, which gravely compromises the breed's future. You may consider requesting the puppy pass a CERF test as part of your purchase agreement.

from Turid Rugaas's book, *On Talking Terms with Dogs: Calming Signals*, Kelly came up with a way to teach Hoosier how to calm himself down during an attack.

Hoosier had already been trained to pay attention when Kelly said his name, so she paired his name with the verbal cue "Get it together" and then added the visual cue of yawning. When an episode started, Kelly would say, "Hoosier, get it together!" and then, when he looked at her, she would take big, slow yawns. After a few yawns, Hoosier's breathing would return to normal. With several years of practice, Hoosier learned how to calm himself and rarely needed the help of Kelly's cues. Instead of having to avoid exercise, he was able to become a successful agility competitor.

PATELLAR LUXATION

Dogs have a kneecap on each hind leg, located at the joint nearest the flank. Patellar luxation occurs when the kneecap moves out of place. When the patellar ligament luxates, a "pop" can be felt. A subluxating patella is a kneecap that is unstable but does not slip out of its joint. Although a luxating patella can be caused by trauma, most patellar luxation has genetic roots. Typically, dogs with less angulation in their back legs are more susceptible. Other contributing factors can be a too-shallow femoral groove or a bowed leg. In those cases, the ligaments holding the patella in place may become damaged. The ligaments themselves may also be weak. Any or all of these conditions will lead to problems. Obesity makes matters all the worse.

Surgery is usually required when the patella becomes loose and pops in and out on its own; in some cases, you are able to pop the kneecap back into place by hand, but manipulating the kneecap doesn't work in the most severe cases. Recovery time can be six weeks or longer and includes exercise restrictions and possibly physical therapy.

HEMIVERTEBRAE

Short, "corkscrew" tails, as seen sometimes in Boston Terriers, Bulldogs, French Bulldogs, and Pugs, result from a deformity of the vertebrae at the tail; this condition is known as hemivertebrae or "butterfly" vertebrae. Affected vertebrae are wedge-shaped, whereas normal vertebrae are cylindrical. As long as the misshapen vertebrae are present only in the tail, which is the usual case with brachycephalic dogs, the dog will not have problems. Sometimes, though, a vertebra can be so misshapen that it affects the spinal cord and causes pain, movement difficulties, or even paralysis. Hemivertebrae is a congenital problem, meaning that puppy is born with it rather than acquiring it sometime during his life as the result of injury or disease.

CANINE ARTHRITIS

Arthritis is very common in Boston Terriers; it can affect Bostons of any age but is often part of the aging process. Arthritis is a degenerative joint disease that is sometimes caused by injury or an underlying condition but usually results from a lifetime of wear and tear. Symptoms include joint pain, heat or swelling around a joint, sensitivity to touch, and stiffness. You may notice changes in your Boston's movement, such as his being hesitant to walk or favoring an affected limb.

Glucosamine and chondroitin are often-recommended supplements for reducing arthritis symptoms, and some veterinarians prescribe anti-inflammatory drugs for pain relief. You should encourage your arthritic Boston to exercise in ways that don't cause him pain. An affected dog must be kept at a healthy weight, as extra weight puts stress on the joints; in fact, keeping your Boston at the proper weight from the outset is a good preventive measure against arthritis.

ALLERGIES

Just as people can have allergies, so can your Boston Terrier; in fact, many of the same allergens—including pollen, dust mites, mold, certain foods, grasses or weeds, flea saliva, and perhaps chemical cleaners or other household products—can affect dogs and people. Allergic reactions include discharge from the nose and/or eyes, sneezing, skin irritation, and digestive issues. Watch for symptoms such as excessive scratching, raw skin or bare patches of your dog's coat, and signs of stomach upset.

One clue to determining which allergens affect your dog is to look at the timing of his allergic reactions. Do they happen year round? That could indicate that mold, dust, or something else in the home is the

Keep an eye on your short-nosed Boston for any signs of overheating or other breathing problems.

Anyone who owns a Boston Terrier with a too-short nose can expect issues that are directly proportional to the shortness of the dog's snout. The dog owner needs to educate him- or herself about what can trigger an episode and what precautions need to be taken, such as not letting the dog get overheated.

—Jan Jensen, DVM, a veterinarian at Palmer Lake Veterinary Clinic in Palmer Lake, Colorado

problem. If he suffers from a seasonal allergy, it could be due to pollen.

You will usually work with your veterinarian to help isolate and resolve the problem. If your vet prescribes corticosteroids right off the bat, you may want to try other options first. Although topical or oral corticosteroids do indeed reduce inflammation, they make a better short-term solution, as long-term usage has undesirable side effects.

Antihistamines can be used with relative safety in dogs, although not all dogs respond to them, and they can have a sedative effect. Some people have tried allergy shots (or immunotherapy) over a period of time in hopes of easing allergic reactions, and this has helped some dogs. Specialized shampoos, such as those made with oatmeal, can also help. If your Boston has a food allergy, you will have to try different foods to isolate the allergic ingredient and eliminate it from his diet. Corn, soy, wheat, and certain preservatives are not the only food items that can cause issues, but they are some of the most common. Many dog owners are finding success with holistic treatments.

INTERNAL PARASITES

Unfortunately, dogs are quite susceptible to internal parasites, often referred to collectively and colloquially as "worms," and some of these worms can infect people. Since the eggs of most worms are expelled in an infected dog's feces, keeping your yard clean and being careful when picking up after your dog are important.

Roundworms

Roundworms are the most common internal parasites. Almost all puppies have roundworms because puppies become infested in utero, meaning while the mother is pregnant. Specialized puppy dewormers are available to help eliminate worms in young dogs, and deworming medications are available for adult dogs, too.

Roundworms live in the intestines and shed eggs continuously. Slender, long, noodle-shaped worms can be found in the stool of a heavily infested dog, or a fecal exam done by a veterinarian will reveal roundworm eggs. Eggs in dirt can remain viable for a while, waiting for a host to ingest them. Young children who play outdoors and get dirt in their mouths often become victims of roundworms from an infected dog. A deworming program prescribed by your vet along with a clean yard will help control roundworm issues.

Hookworms

Hookworms are small worms that hook onto the host's intestinal walls and consume large amounts of blood. Due to their sharp teeth, these worms also cause bleeding in the intestines. Hookworms can be the cause of severe anemia due to iron deficiency. A hookworm infestation can kill a puppy before the eggs are ever discovered in a fecal exam. It is extremely important to test the mother for hookworms because infective larvae are passed from the mother to the puppies through her milk.

Hookworms are very contagious not only to other pets but also to humans. The prevalence of hookworm infections varies with climatic conditions; however, they are present in all parts of the United States and must be viewed as a potential public health hazard. Puppies infected with hookworm need to be treated early to avoid complications, anemia, and possible death. Hookworms are not visible to the naked eye and therefore must be diagnosed by a vet.

As certain types of parasite eggs can survive in the environment after being shed, keeping your Boston's outdoor areas clean is a necessary preventative measure.

A dog infected with hookworm experiences bloody stool, anemia, weight loss, pale gums, diarrhea, and low energy. Skin irritation can also signal a severe hookworm infestation. As a preventive measure, use disposable gloves and a shovel or other type of excrement-disposal device to minimize exposure. Don't allow children to play in areas where dogs have eliminated.

Tapeworms

The common dog tapeworm (*Dipylidium caninum*) is transmitted through fleas. Other tapeworm species use small mammals as intermediate hosts; dogs who catch and eat rabbits, for example, are especially susceptible. Sometimes you can see signs of an infestation in the form of egg sacs around the dog's anus. These sacs look like grains of rice that may or may not be moving. Sometimes you may notice egg sacs in expelled feces, where they may appear larger. If you suspect an infestation, your veterinarian can prescribe a deworming medication. It is uncommon for humans to become infested with dog tapeworm unless they directly ingest fleas, but the less common *Echinococcus multilocularis* can cause severe problems in people. You must practice good hygiene when cleaning up after an infected dog. Flea prevention can lessen your dog's risk of a tapeworm infestation.

Whipworms

Another common worm found in North America is the whipworm. These parasites can cause stomach upset, colic, flatulence, mucus in the stool, and diarrhea. Whipworms are long, thin (whip-shaped) worms that live in the dog's colon and are not visible to the naked eye. They are ingested by the dog, and they attach themselves to the intestinal walls to feed, which in turn causes intestinal bleeding. Although whipworms are the most difficult worms to eliminate, effective treatments are available. The treatment lasts for up to five days and is repeated after several weeks, and possibly again a month or two later. After the dog's treatment is finished, the vet may recommend a monthly heartworm preventive, which protects the dog from future infestations.

A big part of eliminating whipworms is cleaning. Dogs can shed whipworm eggs in their stools for months after treatment, so be fastidious about picking up after your dog in your yard and of course in public places so other dogs don't become infected. Don't let your dog play in areas where he eliminates.

Threadworms

Threadworms can infest dogs and people. They are less common than roundworms and hookworms and are seen primarily in the Southwest and in other states with hot, humid climates. Only female threadworms reach maturity, and they live in the host animal's intestines, where they lay eggs that require no fertilization to hatch into larvae. The host then passes the larvae out of the body in its feces, where the larvae may develop into either free-living worms or parasitic larvae. The parasitic larvae enter a new

The Boston's facial structure and large eyes predispose him to some breed-specific problems, but most Bostons are healthy dogs with active lives.

host by burrowing into its skin. They then move to the lungs and up the trachea to be swallowed by the host animal. When the larvae reach the intestinal tract, they develop into worms, and the cycle begins again. Threadworms can be particularly fatal in puppies. Since they spread easily from animal to animal, threadworms can be a serious problem in kennels or other places where many dogs are in close contact. Although threadworms can't live in colder climates, dogs that come from areas in which threadworms are problematic can pose an unexpected risk to owners in the summer months. Sick puppies must be isolated and treated immediately.

Heartworms

A single mosquito bite can transmit heartworm to your dog. Heartworm larvae transferred into a dog's bloodstream will incubate there for several days. Once hatched, the worms migrate to the heart, where they take up residence.

Adult heartworms can grow to 5 to 6 inches long and live mostly in the heart and the large blood vessel that brings oxygen-rich blood from the lungs to the heart. Adult worms living in the dog's heart produce thousands of microscopic offspring, which then circulate throughout the dog's body. Although these immature worms do not grow to adulthood inside the dog, mosquitoes can ingest them when they bite the dog, and the worms can then complete the development needed to infect another dog.

The best treatment is prevention, which starts with a diagnostic blood test. If your dog is heartworm-free, the vet will put him on a monthly heartworm preventive to protect him from infestation. If your dog tests positive for heartworm, then his fate is quite different. Dogs can recover from heartworm, but treatment is complicated. Medication and painful injections to prevent bacterial damage are administered to the dog, and the vet will restrict the dog's activity, as heartworms can clog the arteries. Heartworms, left untreated, are fatal. Dogs of any age who do not receive heartworm preventives can fall prey to infestation.

Giardia

At one time, gurgling streams offered fresh water for both humans and animals to drink. Unfortunately, due to contamination of water sources by sewage and animal feces, what may look like clean water can contain *Giardia*. *Giardia* is not a worm, but a microorganism that causes gastrointestinal distress. Some dogs and humans will harbor this organism and remain symptom-free. Others will experience bloating, diarrhea, and possibly vomiting days or weeks after exposure. Although a stool-sample analysis can confirm the presence of organism, false negatives are not unusual, meaning that *Giardia* is present but does not show up in the lab results. So a negative test may need to be coupled with clinical signs, and medical history to confirm *Giardia* as the cause of a dog's intestinal problems. An affected dog's feces are often abnormal, with a pale color, unpleasant odor, and greasy appearance. Antibiotics are typically used to treat this problem.

EXTERNAL PARASITES

External parasites lurk in the environment, looking for opportunities to attach themselves to your pet. While most of these parasites can cause problems such as poor coat, itching, and allergic reactions, ticks can transmit serious diseases to your dog.

Be on the lookout for unwanted passengers on your Boston's skin and coat after time spent outdoors.

Fleas

Fleas are tiny wingless insects that feed on dogs, cats, and other animals. When fleas attack a dog, their bites can sometimes trigger an allergic reaction that leaves the dog so miserable that he bites and scratches himself raw. Other dogs merely kick and scratch with their legs, working to get at the biting fleas. If your dog is scratching excessively, inspect the itchy areas for fleas. The quicker you discover fleas and begin treatment to eliminate them from your dog, the easier the task will be. If your flea population gets out of control, you may discover hungry fleas on your own skin, commonly on the wrists and ankles, leaving small, red, itchy bumps behind.

When inspecting your dog for fleas, separate the coat to look at the skin. Fleas are dark-colored bugs about the size of sesame seeds; sometimes you can see them scurrying about on the skin. Common areas to find fleas include the base of the ears, the rump, and areas with less coat, such as the groin. If you don't see live fleas, check for other evidence. Tiny black specks about the size of poppy seeds are flea feces, which are composed of digested blood and will turn reddish in color if you wet them.

If your dog has fleas, you need to eliminate them from the dog and from your environment. There are a range of products, from shampoos to sprays, formulated to kill fleas. Flea collars help keep fleas from returning, but more widely used are topical preventives, typically applied to a small area of the dog's skin once a month. You will need to clean your carpets, the dog's bed, and your furniture. Begin with a thorough vacuuming, and discard the bag when you are finished. Next, treat the areas to kill the fleas. Be aware that different products kill fleas at different stages of development, so be prepared to do a follow-up treatment after the eggs have

Always have your vet's and an emergency clinic's contact info close at hand.

hatched. Follow the instructions and all safety precautions included with the product to ensure that you're using it properly and for the most effective flea elimination. A yard or kennel spray may be used to kill fleas outdoors.

Mites and Mange

Mange is caused by parasitic mites that embed themselves into the dog's hair follicles or skin and cause mayhem, including patches of hair loss and severe itchiness. Demodectic mange (also called *demodicosis* or *red mange*) and sarcoptic mange (or *scabies*) are two types of mange that commonly affect dogs.

Demodectic mange is not considered a contagious disease, and isolation of affected dogs is generally not necessary. The *Demodex* mite lives on the dog as a natural part of the skin's flora without causing problems. However, should the dog become ill or stressed, these organisms can increase in number and cause a mange outbreak. Why some dogs develop demodicosis and others don't is not understood. Many experts feel that that affected dogs have an inherited immune-system defect that makes it difficult for their bodies to keep the mites under control.

Demodectic mange can be either localized or generalized. Localized demodicosis usually occurs in dogs younger than a year, and treatment includes bathing with antibacterial shampoo and applying topical medication. If a dog develops generalized demodicosis over larger areas of the body, more aggressive and lengthier treatment is usually required, including antibiotics for a dog who develops secondary skin infections. Dogs who have recurring or hard-to-cure demodicosis are not recommended for breeding. Although this form of mange is not an inherited condition, the suppressed immune system that allows the dog to be susceptible to the mites can be.

Canine scabies or sarcoptic mange is caused by the parasite *Sarcoptes scabiei*. These microscopic mites can invade the skin of healthy dogs or puppies and create a variety of skin problems, which, as with demodectic mange, include hair loss and severe itching. Sarcoptic mange is contagious to other dogs and to humans, either through direct contact or through the environment. Humans can be infected with this kind of mange, although the mites prefer to live on dogs. There are several effective treatments for scabies. One common method starts with bathing the dog in a benzoyl peroxide shampoo to cleanse the skin, followed by an organophosphate dip. The environment must also be treated to rid the home of mites.

Lice

Lice are flat, wingless insects that are visible to the naked eye. Dog lice do not infect humans, but they can be transmitted from dog to dog. There are two kinds of lice that infect dogs: one type sucks the dog's blood, while the other type chews the skin. Lice lay eggs, called *nits*, on the dog's hair shafts. The life cycle takes about twenty-one days to complete. Lice are the easiest dog parasite to eliminate. Medicated shampoo kills the adult lice, and a repeat treatment ten to fourteen days later will kill the nits that have hatched into adults.

Ticks

Ticks are arachnids. The over 800 tick species are classified into one of two families based upon their structure: *Ixodidae* are hard-shelled ticks, and *Argasidae* are soft-shelled ticks. Ticks suck the dog's blood and can spread diseases, including Rocky Mountain spotted fever and Lyme disease. Ticks usually crawl or drop onto your dog when you are out in a wooded area where the ticks live. Tick collars and monthly topical solutions are among the preventive products available.

To help prevent tick-related problems, do a thorough inspection, wearing latex gloves to protect yourself, of the dog's skin and coat after any time spent in grassy or wooded areas. If you discover a tick, remove it promptly and carefully. If the tick is already engorged, grasp it with tweezers as close to the point of attachment as possible. Pull the tick straight out of the dog without squeezing it. Your goal is to remove the entire tick intact. Dispose of the tick in rubbing alcohol; you may wish to save it in a closed container for further identification in case a problem arises. Wash the site of attachment with soap and water, and watch it for any redness or signs of infection. Tick-borne diseases can take some time, even months, to manifest, so keep an eye on your dog and contact your veterinarian if any symptoms occur.

G ood nutrition benefits your Boston Terrier at all stages of his life. When selecting dog food, basing your choice on price and what you've heard in advertisements is not the most reliable way to pick the best diet for your Boston. You need to learn about canine nutrition and how to read dog food labels, as well as do a little trial and error to find what works well for your dog.

BASIC TYPES OF DOG FOOD

In addition to the myriad brands and formulations out there, you will also have to choose which type of food to feed your dog. If you go the route of traditional packaged dog food, you'll find three main types: dry, wet, and semi-moist.

Dry

Many people find dry dog food the most convenient type of food to feed. The nutritional value of dry dog food varies widely. If you choose dry food for your dog, make sure you get a premium brand made with quality ingredients. Be sure to get the smaller kibble size for your Boston. Some dogs do well if you soak the dry food with water fifteen minutes before serving.

it's a **Fact**

Some states enforce their own labeling regulations for dog food, in addition to those which are set by the Center for Veterinary Medicine and the AAFCO.

Unused portions of canned dog food need to be covered and refrigerated. Dry dog food needs to be sealed tightly to preserve the quality and freshness of the food. One way to do this is to keep dry food in air-tight storage containers, which will help keep out bugs and moisture. Dry dog food can spoil in the summer heat if it is stored improperly.

Wet

Some people prefer to feed their dogs wet, or canned, dog food, as dogs seem to enjoy the taste and moist texture. Other owners mix canned food in with kibble for a little variety and extra flavor. For the most part, canned foods, even those of better quality, tend to cause gas in Bostons and thus are not the best choice. If you try canned food, keep an eye on your dog and only continue feeding the food if your dog does well on it.

Semi-moist

Semi-moist food often comes in tear-open packets and resembles small chunks of meat. This type of dog food usually contains a lot of preservatives and more sugar than other types of food. For these reasons, semi-moist food may not be the best choice as a regular part of your dog's diet.

TRIAL AND ERROR

The Boston Terrier is known to be a gassy breed. This is a problem that is often directly related to what your dog eats. Heavier meats, such as beef and chicken, may not work as well for some Bostons,

given their tendency toward digestive upset. Fish, salmon, and lamb are often better protein sources for Boston Terriers. Likewise, dogs of any breed can suffer from food allergies.

You may need to experiment with different dog foods to find a brand that suits your Boston. No two dogs are guaranteed to do equally well on the same food. When trying a new dog food, you may find that you need to switch your dog gradually from one food to the next, as switching foods abruptly can cause gastrointestinal problems. Try giving your Boston his usual portion in a ratio of one-quarter new food to three-quarters old food for a few days, and then adjust the ratio to a 50/50 mixture for a few days. The next step is to give three-quarters new food and one-quarter old food. After a little more than a week, you should be completely switched to the new food. Give the new food two weeks after the transition to get an accurate evaluation of how your Boston does on it.

Avoid using treats when trying out different foods with your Boston. Once you feel that you have found a good dog food that agrees with your dog and meets his nutritional needs, you can add some treats to his diet. However, if you have a dog who tends to be gassy, try only one kind of treat at a time. Give each treat a two-week trial period before introducing another kind. Table scraps may cause gassiness, so you will likely find that store-bought treats made with quality ingredients will agree with your Boston better than tidbits from your kitchen table.

HOW MUCH TO FEED

How much you should feed your Boston Terrier depends on the dog's age, size, and activity level. A good way to learn

Believe it or not, during your Boston's lifetime, you'll buy a few hundred pounds of dog food! Go to **DogChannel.com/Club-Boston** and download a chart that outlines the cost of dog food.

what works best for your dog is to follow the recommendations from the dog-food manufacturer as indicated on the package and see if your dog maintains a healthy weight. Puppies should eat a puppy-formula food until they are nine months old, at which point they can transition to adult dog food. Senior dogs can do well on a regular adult food unless they have specific health or weight issues that require a specialized food.

You will find that the best way to keep your dog fit and trim is a combination of giving him the right food in the right quantities along with sufficient exercise. To ensure that your dog is getting the right quantity, always measure out the food. Don't leave dry food out for the dog to eat at will, as free-feeding typically leads to obesity. If your dog is a light

eater or a nibbler, try dividing his daily food portion into a number of small meals throughout the day.

WHAT'S IN A NAME?

Our first impression of a dog food often comes from the product's name, and we use this name as part of the criteria by which we evaluate our dog food. Dog-food manufacturers are savvy, and they often appeal to dog owners by including desirable ingredients and carefully chosen adjectives in their product names. The Association of American Feed Control Officials (AAFCO) has set forth rules to govern how products are named based on their ingredients.

1. *The 95 percent rule.* For a product to be called something like "Chicken for Dogs," the food must comprise 95 percent chicken (or whatever the named ingredient is), exclusive of water for processing. Counting the added water, the named ingredient still must account for 70 percent of the product. The named ingredient should appear first in the ingredients list (which lists ingredients in descending order). When a product name contains more than one ingredient, such as "Chicken and Lamb for Dogs," those ingredients must together

Have fresh drinking water out for your Boston at all times.

make up 95 percent of the product's total weight. In this example, there must be more chicken than lamb; the opposite would hold true if the product were called "Lamb and Chicken for Dogs." Most of the foods that fall under the 95 percent rule are canned foods.

2. *The 25 percent rule.* The 25 percent rule, also known as the *dinner rule*, refers to the descriptors that can be used in a product's name. If a food contains at least 25 percent (10 percent when factoring in added water) but less than

95 percent of a main ingredient, it falls under this rule and could be called, for example, "Beef Dinner for Dogs" rather than "Beef for Dogs." Other modifiers, such as *entrée* and *formula*, can be used in place of *dinner*. Similar to the 95 percent rule, if two ingredients are named, then both ingredients must together represent at least 25 percent of the product, with the second ingredient representing at least 3 percent of that 25 percent.

With foods falling under the dinner

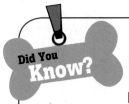

rule, don't expect the named ingredients to be listed first in the ingredients list. Read the label to determine the main ingredient in the food so that you know what you're feeding to your dog.

3. *The 3 percent rule.* Also known as the *with rule*, this allows manufacturers to include in the product name ingredients that make up at least 3 percent of the food, as long as the word *with* is used, e.g., "Chicken Dinner with Egg." Pet owners must read labels of such foods carefully to find out what ingredients comprise the bulk of the food.

4. *The flavor rule.* For a dog food to be labeled as "flavored with" a certain ingredient (i.e., beef-flavored or chicken-flavored), it does not have to contain the named ingredient in any specific percentage, but it must have a detectable level, as determined by AAFCO testing methods, of the specified flavor. So as not to deceive consumers, the word *flavor* or *flavored* must be shown on the package in the same font, color, and size as the named ingredient.

Outside of these rules, manufacturers of pet food can use adjectives such as *premium* and *gourmet* without any particular quality standards. The word *natural* does not mean that a food is organic; it generally means that the food was made without artificial preservatives, flavors, or colors, but this is not a term defined by the AAFCO. Any claim on a dog-food package that its contents are "complete and balanced" must be accompanied by an AAFCO nutritional adequacy statement; be sure to look for this on the label. Do not be swayed by the many marketing gimmicks or eye-catching claims that you will see on dog-food packages. Simply read the list of ingredients.

NUTRIENT BREAKDOWN

Proteins serve as building blocks for parts of the body, including tissues, organs, enzymes, and antibodies. Proteins are essential for growth and repair. There are both animal and plant sources of protein. Although the percentage of crude protein in your dog's food will be listed on the package, don't rely on that number alone to evaluate the food. More important are the source and quality of the protein, which you can determine by the ingredient list.

When we think of **fat**, we may envision our veterinarian wagging his finger as he scolds us about our overweight dog. However, fat is not all bad, and it serves several purposes in the canine body. Fat is a form of fuel. In an overweight person or dog, too much fat represents stored fat that is waiting to be burned off, but a certain amount of fat is needed to help support the body's internal organs. When a dog carries around too much "padding" and his ribs become hidden, that extra fat is not healthy and needs to be decreased with exercise and changes to his diet.

Some fats are necessary to maintain health, but they must be supplied in your dog's diet because the body cannot produce them. Essential fatty acids, including omega-3 and omega-6, need to be added as supplements. They are required for normal growth and function of the cells, muscles, nerves, and organs and for the production of hormone-like substances that

Peanut-Butter Dog Biscuits

2½ cups whole-wheat flour

2 eggs

½ cup canned pumpkin

2 Tbsp peanut butter

Mix all ingredients together in a bowl. Add water if needed to make the dough workable, but expect the dough to be dry and stiff. Roll the dough out to a half-inch thickness and use a cookie cutter to cut out shapes. Bake at 350°F for 40 minutes or until brown.

Easy Treats for the Picky Dog

2 cups oats

4 ounces of peeled, cooked, and pureed sweet potatoes/yams or baby-food sweet potatoes

⅔ cup apple juice

Mix together all ingredients and let stand for 5 minutes to let the oats soak up some of the liquid. When the oats are oatmeal-like in consistency, spoon out the mixture onto a greased cookie sheet in small spoonfuls (about half a tablespoon each). Spread each spoonful to be about 1 inch around. Bake in a preheated oven at 375°F for about 15 minutes, until lightly browned. Remove cookies with a spatula and place on a cooling rack to cool.

If your Boston needs to lose some weight, try soaking his portion of dry dog food in water before giving it to him. This will help your dog feel fuller right after he eats.

are key to many important processes in the body. Fatty-acid deficiencies are linked to a variety of health problems, including heart disease, cancer, and diabetes.

Carbohydrates are used as energy in the body. Corn, barley, and white rice are commonly used as carbohydrate sources in dog food, but there are dog foods made with better quality carbohydrates, such as sweet potatoes, brown rice, and whole grains. Carbohydrates that take longer to break down in the body and give more sustained energy are better for dogs (and people, too).

Minerals and **vitamins** are important for nerve function, bone growth, healing, and overall metabolism. Minerals and vitamins are needed in specific amounts, as deficiencies can impact your dog's health and cause poor growth, but high doses can cause toxicity. Some vitamins and minerals are bonded with a substance, such as an amino acid, to help insure adequate absorption.

Fiber comes from indigestible cellulose and provides roughage for normal digestive function.

Water is an often-overlooked nutrient. Dog food contains water in varying amounts; for example, canned food has a higher water content than dry food. Make sure that your Boston has unlimited access to clean, fresh drinking water (but keep a close eye on his water intake during house-training). Good hydration helps promote normal function of the body's systems.

Don't overdo it with treats! Calories add up quickly, especially in smaller dogs like Bostons.

Exactly how much impact pesticides, plastics, parasite medications, vaccinations, hormones, and other assorted toxic materials in the environment have on the well-being of our animals is difficult to determine.

—*from an AKC Gazette article by Patricia Trotter, AKC judge and author of*
Born to Win: Breed to Succeed

READING AND UNDERSTANDING LABELS

To prove a point about how confusing and even misleading pet-food labels can be, a manufacturer made a mock product that included 10 percent protein, 6.5 percent fat, 2.4 percent fiber, and 68 percent moisture, similar to what you see on many canned pet-food labels. The problem was that the ingredients used were old leather work boots, used motor oil, crushed coal, and water. The moral of the story is that you can't rely on percentages alone when evaluating dog food. You need to look at the ingredients list. If a food has a high percentage of protein, but the first ingredient listed is something other than meat, then that food is probably a poor choice because the amount of protein alone doesn't guarantee the digestibility and quality of that protein.

Since ingredients, by law, must be listed in descending order by weight, look for meat as the first ingredient in the listed. Beware of meat meal, as some can be very poor quality. If corn is the second ingredient listed, you are probably looking at a lower quality dog food. Also be cautious of manufacturers that play labeling games, which can help disguise the fact that corn or another grain is actually higher in quantity than meat. For example, if the first ingredient is meat, but the next few are corn meal, corn bran, and corn middlings, then by weight you have more total corn than meat. Manufacturers have learned to split up corn and rice into their components when labeling to give the illusion of less total quantity of these ingredients. Don't be fooled.

STAGES OF LIFE

Manufacturers formulate dog food for many different stages of life. Regulators of dog food, however, recognize only two stages: growth and maintenance. Growth-formula dog food is what you feed your puppy until he is mature; Boston Terriers are usually kept on puppy food until around nine months of age. When you switch to an adult food, you'll need a good maintenance formula. So if you have a non-breeding dog with a normal activity level and no health problems that require specialized dog food, he should do fine on a quality maintenance food. Foods for stages other than growth and maintenance are not regulated to guarantee specific nutrients and must be considered on their own merit.

SNACKS AND TREATS

Snacks and treats are intended for supplemental feeding only. They are not regulated as far as nutritional requirements. Many treats are made to appeal to people in their appearance, but choosing treats that have eye appeal rather than nutrition is not good for your dog. Make sure that treats are more than just artificial flavors and colors. Choose snacks and treats that have quality natural ingredients, and use them sparingly. When given in excess, treats can become the catalyst of a weight problem. You can break snacks into smaller pieces so that you can reward your dog more often without overfeeding him.

Diet Dos and Don'ts

Dogs of all ages love treats and table food, but these goodies can unbalance your dog's diet and lead to a weight problem if not fed wisely. Extra morsels, whether fed as treats or as part of a meal, shouldn't account for more than 10 percent of your dog's daily caloric intake.

When shopping for packaged treats, look for ones with nutritional value. Choose crunchy goodies for chewing fun and dental health. Tasty treats you might have at home include:

- small chunks of cooked, lean meat
- morsels of dry dog food
- small bits of cheese
- veggies (cooked, raw, or frozen)
- breads, crackers, or dry cereal
- unsalted, unbuttered, plain popcorn

Some foods that people eat can pose hazards for dogs, ranging from mild gastrointestinal upset to severe illness and even death:

- **avocados:** in sufficient quantity, these can cause gastrointestinal irritation, with vomiting and diarrhea
- **baby food:** don't feed any baby foods that contain onion powder
- **cat food:** can cause diarrhea in some dogs, and will most likely cause gas in your Boston; it is generally too high in protein and fat for your dog
- **chocolate:** contains methylxanthines and theobromine, caffeine-like compounds that can cause vomiting, diarrhea, heart abnormalities, tremors, seizures, and death; darker chocolates contain higher levels of the toxins
- **eggs (raw):** may contain salmonella, and the whites contain an enzyme that prevents uptake of biotin, a B vitamin
- **garlic (and related foods):** can cause gastrointestinal irritation and anemia if eaten in sufficient quantity
- **grapes, raisins, and currants:** can cause kidney failure if eaten in sufficient quantity
- **macadamia nuts:** can cause vomiting, weakness, lack of coordination, and other problems
- **meat (raw):** may contain harmful bacteria such as salmonella or E. coli
- **milk and other dairy products:** can cause diarrhea in some puppies
- **mushrooms:** can contain toxins, which may affect multiple body systems, cause shock, and result in death—this pertains especially to mushrooms found in your yard or in wooded areas
- **onions (and related foods):** can cause gastrointestinal irritation and anemia if eaten in sufficient quantity; in smaller dogs, such as Boston Terriers, too much can cause death, and the effects can accumulate over days
- **fatty meats, fat trimmings, poultry skin:** many fatty foods can cause pancreatitis
- **yeast bread dough:** can rise in the gastrointestinal tract, causing obstruction; produces alcohol as it rises
- **xylitol:** this artificial sweetener can cause very low blood sugar (hypoglycemia), insulin shock, and liver failure

The Boston Terrier is one of the easiest breeds when it comes to grooming—that short, sleek coat seems to keep itself in order. However, even short coats benefit from brushing, and any dead hairs will accumulate in the brush, not on your furniture or in corners around the house. And an occasional bath is a good idea to freshen your Boston up.

Grooming includes trimming your dog's nails. Even if you tend to take your Boston on a lot of walks, his nails will typically grow faster than they can be worn down by walking on pavement and other hard surfaces. Clean teeth are important for good health; brushing your Boston's teeth will also be part of your regular grooming routine. If your Boston has a lot of folds around his face, which is common in dogs with short snouts, then you will need to clean those folds with a soft washcloth every few days.

TIME TO GROOM

Routine grooming tasks help you maintain a Boston Terrier who looks and feels good. By starting when your dog is young and working with him on a regular basis, grooming will be less of a chore.

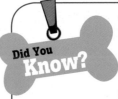

Did You Know? The earlier you start routine grooming tasks with a dog, the easier it will be for him to accept them. Just go at the dog's pace and never do anything to frighten him.

he's closer to the ground than many other breeds. Brushing with a soft bristle brush can help remove unwanted pollen and dust. To help remove loose hairs before they deposit themselves on your couch or floor, try raking the coat with a fine-toothed stripping comb once a week. The correct way to brush or comb is to stroke in the same direction in which the hair naturally lies.

Brushing also helps maintain the health and shine of your dog's coat. Your dog's hair follicles have glands that produce oil. Brushing distributes the oil, keeping your Boston's coat from drying out as well as keeping his skin supple. Rubber brushes or grooming gloves, which have rounded nubs instead of bristles, are useful to stimulate the skin and coat and can also be used when bathing the dog.

Bathing

There are a variety of shampoos for dogs on the market. For your Boston Terrier, you'll do well to select a shampoo for shorthaired dogs. Also get a puppy shampoo—the tearless variety—to use on the dog's face. There are also many types of conditioner available for dogs' coats; however, Boston

Brushing

Although Boston Terriers shed very little, you still need to brush your Boston. For example, in the spring and summer, his coat will collect pollen, and all year long, his coat can collect dust, especially since

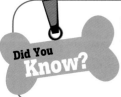

Did You Know?

Ear inspections can help prevent ear infections. If you suspect that a problem is developing, bring it to the attention of your veterinarian. Left untreated, an ear infection can damage your dog's hearing.

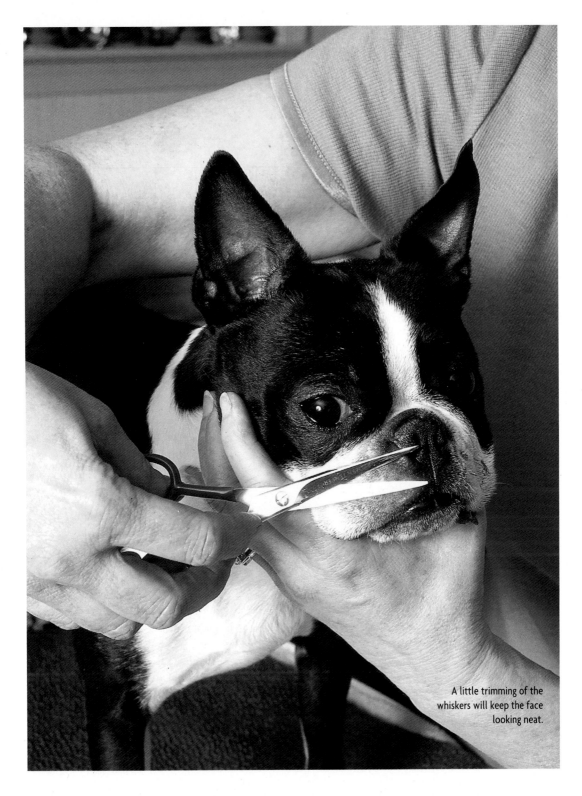

A little trimming of the whiskers will keep the face looking neat.

Terriers don't normally need coat conditioner. In fact, using too much conditioner on a shorthaired dog, such as the Boston Terrier, can sometimes cause flaky skin.

Brush your dog both before and after you bathe him. Brushing him before the bath will remove any loose hair, and brushing him afterward will eliminate additional hairs that were loosened during the bathing process.

When washing your dog, you'll find the process much easier if you can use a spray nozzle to thoroughly soak his coat. Work the shampoo into a good lather and then grab a rubber brush or grooming glove to help stimulate and exfoliate the skin. Before you wash around the face, put some cotton balls into your dog's ears to keep water out. If you notice your dog shaking his head, you may have accidentally gotten some water in his ears. If you suspect that this is the case, be sure to use an ear wash after you are done washing and drying the dog, as this will help remove excess moisture from the ears.

Wash your dog's face with a tearless shampoo, making sure to clean any wrinkles and skin folds. Be sure to rinse these areas extra carefully so that no shampoo is trapped in the wrinkles.

A tearless shampoo for the dog's face will be gentler should you unintentionally get some shampoo in his eyes. If the dog is pawing at his eyes or blinking a lot, use some saline eye wash to rinse his eyes. Saline eye wash can be used at any time to remove irritants from your Boston's eyes.

When it is time to rinse off your dog, be thorough. Rinse until the water runs clean, then rinse again. Shampoo residue can irritate the skin and cause flaking. Be gentle when rinsing your Boston's face so that you don't spray his eyes with water or get water into his ears. Hold your dog's face so that he's looking upward while you rinse.

To dry your Boston, rub him with a clean bath towel. You can then either let the dog air-dry or use a hair dryer made for dogs to finish drying. Be aware that if the dog is even just a little bit damp, he will want to roll around, so don't let the dog go outside until he is completely dry. When the dog is dry, give him a once-over with a soft-bristled brush.

Nail Clipping

Clipping nails is usually one of the dog owner's most dreaded tasks. That very dread makes the dog dread the task also. However, by training the dog correctly, you can make nail trimming just another part of your routine. Start training your Boston to accept nail clipping as a pup. While you are holding your puppy in your lap, enjoying his company, begin to play with his paws. Take one of his paws in your hand and gently apply pressure to it, followed by soothing petting. Separate each digit and give it a gentle wiggle. If your pup fusses at this, stop and talk affectionately to him. After your Boston settles down, again hold his paw briefly, then talk to him a little and end the session. Work with your dog until he becomes comfortable with your handling all of his paws and manipulating all of his digits.

Ideally, the breeder has already done a few nail trims. If so, the dog should be

it's a
Fact

It is not safe to use human toothpaste for dogs; dogs need their own specially formulated toothpaste.

Always be careful when cleaning your Boston's ears that you never probe into the ear canal.

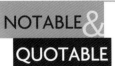

This is a fairly easy breed to take care of. I bathe [my Boston Terriers] every two weeks and have really never had any coat problems. I don't use any type of specialty shampoo, just a dog shampoo.

—Irene Kruse, Boston Terrier owner from Colorado Springs, Colorado

the back paws. If your dog shows apprehension about having his nails trimmed, just take a little bit off the tip of one nail, comforting him with petting and soothing talk as and after you snip. It is fine to only take a snip or two the first time if the dog is nervous. You don't need to complete the job in one sitting, but you do need to teach the dog to relax when his nails are being clipped. So rather than go for quantity, just do a few nails and make sure that you can settle the dog down after each one. Work up to doing a few more nails at a time in subsequent sessions.

A lot of people wonder just how much to trim off of the nails. If you nip too much, you can cut into the quick (which you can see in lighter colored nails), which bleeds and will be painful for the dog. In dark-nailed dogs, it can be hard to determine just how much to take off. Some people have found that using a light behind the nail helps determine where the quick is. When in doubt, just take off a little bit. After a week, you can take off a little more, because the quick will recede away from the end of the nail. Continue with small snips until you've cut the nails down to the desired length.

Some owners prefer to use a small battery-operated nail grinder with their Boston Terriers, feeling that the grinder enables them to shorten the nail more gradually and thus reduce the risk of cutting the quick. Other owners simply bring

used to little snips. Be ready with a pair of small nail clippers made for dogs. When you introduce your dog to nail trimming, begin with one of the back paws. Dogs tend to fuss less when you begin with

Did You Know?

Nail grinders come in heavy-duty and light-duty types. If using a grinder with your Boston Terrier, choose a battery-powered light-duty model. Introduce him to the grinder by turning it on and letting him get used to the noise before you touch his nails with it.

The well-groomed Boston has a neat appearance and sleek, shiny coat.

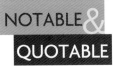

NOTABLE & QUOTABLE

Cat nail clippers are easier to use on little dogs than big dog clippers. Some people also find that dogs are more receptive to nail trims using an electric nail grinder.

—Linda Bollinger, owner of Brightmeadow Grooming in Palmer Lake, Colorado

their dogs to their groomers or veterinarians for nail trimming as the need arises.

Teeth

Some toothbrushes for dogs have long handles and bristles, similar to those made for people; others fit on the owner's fingertip and may have bristles or rubber nubs. Both types do the trick, so pick one that's easy for you to work with and that your dog doesn't mind. Also get toothpaste formulated for dogs; many of them come in special flavors to entice your dog.

Dogs need to have their teeth brushed on a regular basis to keep their teeth and gums healthy. Just as with nail trimming, it is best to get into the habit when the dog is young. To introduce the dog to brushing, you can put a small amount of toothpaste on your finger and rub his teeth with your finger. When the dog gets used to this, try using the toothbrush. The first couple of times, stroke the teeth only once or twice. You can slowly work up to more thorough brushings over time. Brush your dog's teeth twice a week; if he has dental issues, you may need to brush them more often.

Ears

Look inside your Boston's ears for dirt, and use a little liquid ear wash on a cotton ball to spot-clean them if necessary; your veterinarian can recommend a good ear-wash product. Your Boston's ears should look and smell clean. If there is an odor, you should have your dog's ears checked by your veterinarian. If water or anything else gets into your dog's ear, it is important to get it out as soon as possible so that the dog doesn't end up with an infection that requires veterinary care.

To use an ear wash for a more thorough cleaning or to help dry up water in your Boston's ear, measure out the suggested amount and pour it into the dog's ear. Press down on the outer part of the ear to trap the fluid inside, then massage the ear area to distribute the ear wash inside the ear. Your dog will probably shake his head after the administration of the ear wash. The ear wash will dry out on its own and will also dry up any excess moisture inside the ear.

Eyes

Eye wash is also good to have on hand, especially with a Boston. Gentle saline solution—the type available for people—works well. Get a large bottle so that you can use it liberally should you need to wash something out of your dog's eyes.

It is a good idea to check your Boston's eyes on a daily basis. If your dog has a lot of dry matter around his eyelids, apply a drop or two of eye wash to the eyes, then use a soft cloth or dry cotton ball to carefully wipe the corners. If your dog has white coat around the eyes, and it becomes tear-stained, apply a tear-stain remover to the affected areas, being careful not to get it in the dog's eyes. If your Boston seems to be tearing excessively and is constantly wet under the eyes, or if you notice unusual redness or swelling in or around the eyes, consult your vet.

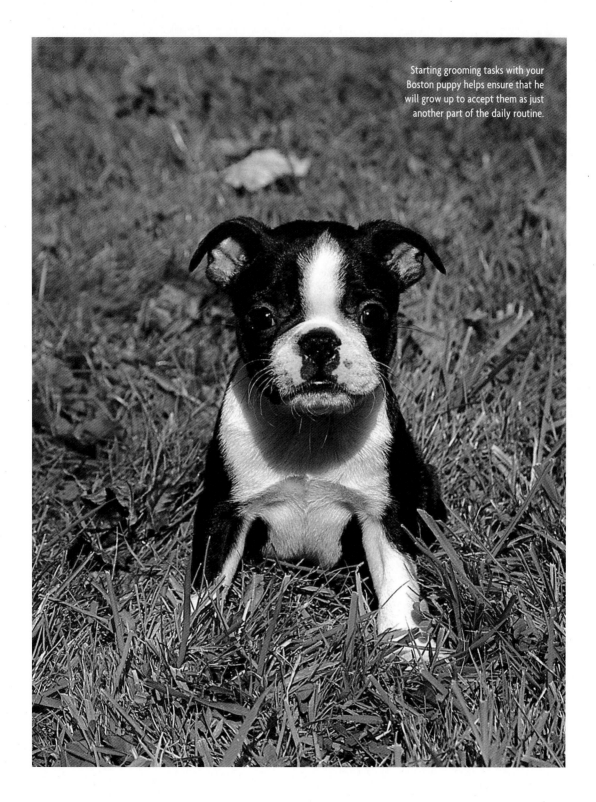

Starting grooming tasks with your Boston puppy helps ensure that he will grow up to accept them as just another part of the daily routine.

LOOKING FOR A GROOMER

Some people prefer to take their dogs to groomers rather than do it themselves. If you're one of those people, here are some tips about how to find a good groomer.

When shopping for a groomer, shop wisely. Call ahead and make an appointment to meet with the groomer and see the salon before you bring in your Boston. Talk with the groomer and be sure that you are comfortable with his or her demeanor. Look around the area. Is it kept relatively clean? Will the groomer let you take a look at the cages, or does the groomer want you to stay in the reception area only? When you look at the grooming cages where animals are kept, take note to see if the animals look stressed.

Ask the groomer what services are included in the price. Some groomers do a basic bathing and brushing and charge extra for cleaning teeth, expressing glands, and trimming nails; others offer packages that include these additional services. Ask what kind of shampoo the groomer uses on Boston Terriers. He or she should tell you why a specific shampoo is used. Ask your groomer if he or she has a special puppy introductory rate, as most do.

Even before your puppy needs grooming, take him in to the groomer's salon to help him get used to the experience. That way, the young dog learns at a relaxed pace to become comfortable with the

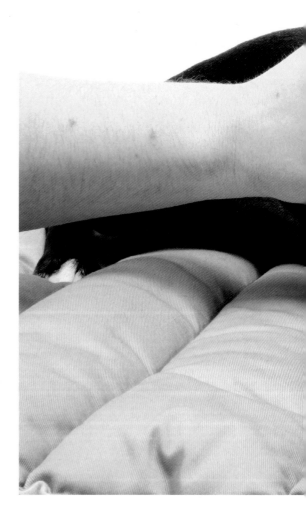

If you choose to groom your Boston yourself, which many owners do, it can be a bonding experience for you and your dog.

Tips from a Groomer

- Don't use a human hair dryer on your Boston Terrier, as it can get too hot. Instead, invest in a hair dryer made for dogs.

- If your Boston has wrinkles and folds on his face, you will need to keep those areas clean in between baths. Use a soft washcloth and a little soap and water. Be sure to rinse away all soap residue and dry the areas well. If you see chafing or any other issues, talk to your veterinarian.

- During times of shedding, brush your Boston more frequently to get rid of dead hairs.

- If your dog is very apprehensive about having his nails clipped, hold the dog in your lap and make a clipping noise without actually cutting. When you finally clip one nail, follow it immediately with a treat and praise.

- Whether you use a bathtub or sink to bathe your dog, don't leave him unattended, even for a moment. This can be dangerous, especially if you have him tethered and he tries to jump.

- Although most Bostons don't have tear-staining issues, if yours does, you can buy special wipes to help remove the stains. Although there are anti-tear-stain supplements that you can add to your dog's food or drinking water, don't use these products without first checking with your veterinarian.

entire process, thus creating an adult dog who doesn't become stressed when taken to a groomer. The best time to introduce your puppy or new adult dog to a groomer is anytime after he has finished his series of vaccinations.

When you do bring in your dog, see how the groomer acts. If the groomer is paying more attention to you than to your Boston, beware. Groomers should love animals and do this job as a passion. Good groomers almost have to remind themselves to pay attention to the people, too, as they really care about animals and are usually engrossed in spending time with their four-legged customers.

Every Boston Terrier deserves to look beautiful. What do you need to keep your dog looking terrific? Go to Club Boston (**DogChannel. com/Club-Boston**) and download a checklist of essential grooming equipment that you and your dog will need.

The Boston Terrier in general is a relatively easy-to-train breed. Many Bostons simply live to please. However, as with any breed, individuals can have unique characteristics, and some Bostons may have more of the bully-breed willfulness or the terrier "mind of their own" than others.

SOCIALIZING YOUR BOSTON

Socialization means introducing your dog to people outside your immediate family, other dogs, and all types of experiences. Socializing your Boston is essential and must be done with care. Begin socializing your Boston as early as possible. It is hoped that your puppy's breeder began some of the pup's socialization while the litter was still together. Dogs younger than eight weeks of age who are introduced to children and a variety of adults get a good head start on their socialization. Once your puppy is home, the continued socialization falls on your shoulders. Keep introducing your dog to different people as much as

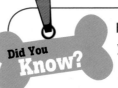

Did You Know?

How you approach your training can facilitate success or create training problems. Although some breeds may tolerate punishment and harsh training techniques, such as using a choke chain for corrections, the Boston responds best to positive training.

When socializing your Boston Terrier, quality gets the job done more than quantity. Make sure that every social experience ends on a positive note, even if you only do a few introductions.

possible during this most critical socialization period, which lasts through fourteen weeks of age. After that time, socialization is still very important, but you will not need to work as hard at it. If you miss this early socialization period, if you've adopted an adult, or if your Boston has a shyer nature, you will also need to put in some extra effort to adequately socialize your dog.

When socializing your Boston, always supervise the process, especially with children. Small children can unintentionally be too rough with a puppy, so don't leave them together unattended, even for a moment. If you can't convince the child to handle your dog gently, then hold your dog while you show the child the correct way to pet the dog.

If you have a Boston who seems a bit timid around people and just doesn't warm up quickly, take it slowly and give him extra time with each person he meets—don't merely make a quick introduction to a person and move on to the next. In fact, if your dog is on the shy side, briefly meeting a lot of people can become too overwhelming for him, leaving him feeling more insecure. What works better is to introduce your Boston to a person and allow them to spend some time together. Once the dog has relaxed, then and only then can you move on to another person. Although the time involved may limit how many people

you can introduce your dog to in one session, this actually works to your advantage so that your dog doesn't meet too many people in too little time. As the dog becomes less timid, he will be able to tolerate more people. By taking introductions at your dog's pace, you will leave the dog with the right impression about meeting strangers.

When socializing your young Boston with other dogs, you can find a lot of playmates of the same age at a puppy class. However, some more rambunctious dogs can overwhelm shyer ones. If you have a less outgoing Boston, ask to have your puppy put in a group with other pups who are more reserved. By working to help shape your dog's social nature at a young age and in appropriate ways, you are creating a confident dog who is easy to take anywhere.

TRAINING BASICS

Many people wonder why they should bother teaching their dogs to sit or lie down. These simple commands have value in setting up communication between you and your dog. When you approach basic training correctly, the dog not only learns to do as he is told but also to look to you for guidance. Although many Bostons love to please their owners, any dog will want to do his own thing—rather than what his owner expects of him—at times.

The process of having your dog obey a command, or cue, is the beginning of setting ground rules and giving your dog boundaries. Training can also communicate what the dog can and can't do. By teaching the dog what you want him to do instead of punishing him for unwanted behaviors, you are training proactively instead of reactively. Since Boston Terriers are sensitive dogs that do not like reprimands and punishment, using positive

Positive-reinforcement training is based on showing the dog what is expected of him through encouragement and rewards.

The best way to get your Boston well socialized is to introduce him to different kinds of people and situations. Have him meet a man with a beard, take him to a dog-friendly restaurant, take him for a ride in the car. Go online to download a socialization checklist at **DogChannel.com/Club-Boston.**

training techniques will promote a happier and healthier relationship with your dog.

CLICKER TRAINING AND SHAPING BEHAVIORS

Clicker training was first used to train dolphins. The method was adopted by dog trainers in the early 1990s, and it has become a popular way to train dogs. Using a clicker helps keep the trainer focused on rewarding the dog for wanted behaviors while ignoring unwanted behaviors. Part of clicker training involves shaping behaviors, meaning that you reward small steps that lead toward the final desired behavior. Once the dog arrives at the final behavior, that behavior is emphasized to help the dog understand what you ultimately are teaching him.

The clicker itself is a small device—usually plastic with a metal piece inside that makes the clicking noise—that you can find at most pet-supply stores. The click tells the dog when he has done something right. To teach the dog that the click means something positive, you pair it with a treat—when the dog performs the desired behavior, you click and immediately offer a treat. Soon the click represents a reward, just like a treat does, to the dog, and you no longer need to give a treat every time you click.

Once the dog associates the click with the idea that what he just did was a good thing, you can begin to use the clicker to *mark* behaviors. For example, if you say "Sit" and the dog plants his rear end, you can click at the moment when the dog's behind lands on the ground, telling the dog that he just did what he's supposed to do. The click marks the behavior that you want. If you say "Sit," and the dog lies down instead, you don't click, communicating to the dog that he did not do what you wanted.

You can also use the clicker to *shape* behaviors, meaning that you click to let the dog know that what he's doing is a step in the direction of the target behavior. Some people use shaping to teach the *down* cue. In this case, you begin by saying "Down." If the dog lowers himself toward the ground, you click as a sign of approval even though he has not fully accomplished the *down*. Often, the dog will try to figure out what he did to get his clicking reward, and thus will try the behavior again. As the dog repeats the behavior, he will likely keep lowering himself closer and closer to the floor. By clicking as the dog moves closer to the ground, he will keep progressing toward that final goal of lying all the way down. When the dog lies down, you mark his accomplishment by giving a higher value reward, such as a click paired with a treat or a favorite toy. The foregoing is a simplified description of clicker-training basics; there are many books, videos, and classes that can help dog owners learn this training technique.

COUNTERCONDITIONING

Counterconditioning describes the process of replacing a negative response to a stimulus with a positive response to the same stimulus. Dog trainers use counter-

it's a **Fact**

Until your dog has completed his puppy shots, be cautious about where you take him for socialization, as you'll need to limit his exposure to situations in which other dogs may expose him to disease.

Food is not the only reward in training. Try offering a favorite toy or engaging your Boston in some interactive play after a job well done.

conditioning to help change unwanted behaviors in dogs. Counterconditioning works to address the unwanted behavior, and instead of disciplining or punishing the dog for his unwanted actions, you teach the dog to do a different behavior. For example, if you have a dog who jumps on you to greet you when you get home, and you want the dog to stop doing that, you must teach the dog a different way to greet you, such as sitting in front of you instead. The dog learns that when he sees you and wants to be greeted, he must sit to be rewarded with your attention. You are changing the dog's original reaction to seeing you from "jump to get attention" to "sit to get attention."

Counterconditioning is often used when dogs are afraid or upset. If your Boston Terrier gets upset when he sees another dog coming down the street, you can teach him to do something other than lunging at the end of the leash. What often works well is to have your dog sit and focus

on you to get a treat. By using this redirection technique, in which you use food to redirect your dog's attention onto you instead of whatever is causing him to react negatively, you're conditioning the dog to react in a neutral or even positive way. To put it another way, you're countercondition his fearful response by changing it into the pleasant experience of getting a treat.

EQUIPMENT

The leash and collar are the traditional equipment used for training. If using a nylon collar, it should be at least an inch wide, as a too-narrow collar can damage your dog's throat if he gets excited and pulls against it. Never use a choke chain or slip collar on your Boston. A quick-clip collar is often more convenient than a buckle collar. A 4- to 6-foot leash works fine; you may want one of each length for different training tasks and walking. An approximately half-inch-wide nylon lead is fine; some people prefer thinner leather leashes, especially if they show their dogs in obedience. For a Boston who tends to grab the leash and chew, a lightweight chain leash is a better option.

INTRODUCING THE LEASH

There are several good ways to accustom your Boston to the leash and teach him some basic manners. Which method works best for your dog depends on his nature and sometimes his mood at the moment. One idea is to attach the leash to the dog's collar and hold the leash loosely while you follow the dog around for a while. This lets the dog know that the leash means that the two of you need to stick together. Another idea is to use a bit of food to lure the dog to keep up with you when his leash is attached. Praise the dog

Your Boston may need a little coaxing to stay at your side and walk at your pace on leash.

With the proper training, your Boston will be as well behaved as he is good-looking. One certification that all dogs should receive is the American Kennel Club's Canine Good Citizen (CGC), which rewards dogs who demonstrate good manners. Go to **DogChannel.com/Club-Boston** and click on "Downloads" to learn about the ten exercises that your dog must complete to earn his CGC.

and give him the treat for coming along. If the dog stops and doesn't want to follow, try applying slight pressure on the leash. When the dog steps forwards, he will be immediately rewarded by the release of pressure. If that works, grab a treat and lure the dog back into motion. You may also try clapping your hands to coax the dog toward you. Never use the leash to drag the dog; that does nothing to train him. Keep your leash lessons short at first, and increase the time gradually.

TEACHING *SIT*

To teach your Boston to sit, stand in front of him and hold a treat just above his nose. Since the dog wants to get that treat, he will keep his eyes on it. Slowly move the treat over his head. As he looks up and back to follow the treat with his eyes, he should end up in the *sit* position. You can encourage his success by saying "Good" as the dog moves his rear end toward the ground. The moment the dog's behind hits the ground, even if he stays in position for only an instant, give the verbal cue "Sit" and then give him that treat.

THE *WATCH* CUE

When a dog makes eye contact with you by glancing at your face or your eyes, he not only is communicating that he is paying attention but he also is acknowledging that you are in charge. The *watch* cue does more than teach the dog to simply look at you—it helps teach your dog the concept of looking to you for guidance.

One way to teach the *watch* cue is to show your dog a treat and say "Watch" as you move that treat up to your eyes. When the dog looks toward your eyes, toss the treat to reward him. The dog will soon learn that to get the treat, he needs to first glance at you.

TEACHING THE *DOWN*

Down is often easier to teach when you start with your Boston in a sitting position. To get started, tell your dog to sit and reward him when he does. Next, use a treat to lure your dog to lower the front of his body toward the floor. Use the word "Good" for every movement that the dog makes toward the floor, and mark the full *down* position with an enthusiastic "Yes" and a treat. Don't strive for perfection the first time. Anything close to lying down should be rewarded. With practice, your dog will figure out what you want him to do, and he should start to lie down more readily. Reward your dog when he reaches the *down* position by feeding him several treats while he remains in position. However, if your dog starts to get up, stop the treats. Only reward the action you want.

TEACHING THE *STAY*

One way to teach a dog to stay is to reward your dog while he is staying and stop rewarding him when he breaks the *stay* or when you release him from the command. This helps increase your Boston's interest in an otherwise boring task. To teach *stay*, place your dog in a *sit* or *down* position. With your hands full of treats, feed one treat at a time to your dog. With each treat, say "Good stay." After a few seconds,

You want your Boston to be focused on you and the lesson during your training sessions.

Anyone who interacts with the dog plays a role in training the dog—whether he or she lives in the home or just stops by to visit. Everyone should have the same expectations and work together to accomplish them.
—Lauren Fox, CPDT-KA, director of All Breed Rescue & Training in Colorado Springs, Colorado

release your dog with your chosen release word, and walk away. "Okay" is a commonly used release word that communicates to your dog that the lesson is over.

In the next lesson, have your dog stay for few more seconds while giving him treats and telling him "Good stay." Add more time, a few seconds at a time, when he is successful. Eventually begin to stretch out the time in between treats, but remember that if your dog breaks the stay, stop the treats. Simply put him back into his *sit* or *down* and restart the lesson.

Once the dog is solid with a one-minute *stay*, begin to take a step away from him, wait a few seconds, and then return and reward him with a treat. Each time you reward the dog with a treat, repeat "Good stay" so that he understands why he just got a treat. Don't reward if your dog breaks his *stay*. He must learn to remain in position until you release him.

After your Boston gets used to your taking one step away, try two steps. Work up to taking several steps away while your dog remains in the *stay*. When your dog becomes comfortable with you a few steps away from him, you can wait a little longer before returning to give him the treat. Go at the dog's pace, but work up to ten seconds between treats, then fifteen seconds, and then only two treats a minute. Don't forget to end the session with your release word, which signals to your dog that he can walk away and that there are no more rewards for staying.

If, at any time during a training session, the dog breaks his *stay*, stop rewarding him and start again at a point at which you had success. By rewarding a successful *stay*, the dog will learn what he needs to do.

TEACHING THE *COME*

Every dog needs a reliable recall, meaning that he consistently responds appropriately to the *come* command. Start your training indoors by calling him to you and then offering him a treat when he reaches you. Get the dog to associate the word "Come" with the idea that you want to either play with him or give him a treat. Practice this throughout the day in different parts of the house.

Once your dog has the idea that coming to you means a reward for him, take him outside, where there are more distractions. Attach a long lead, at least 15 feet, and allow him to become distracted. Call him to come. If he doesn't respond right away, use the leash to guide him to you and reward him when he arrives. When your dog learns to ignore the distractions and come to you without your help, you can remove the leash; do this first in a securely fenced area until you're sure of his response.

Once the dog gets into the habit of coming when called, you can phase out the rewards. However, it doesn't hurt to remind him that coming when called is a good thing by every so often offering him a reward even after he's reliable with the recall; continuing to reward him intermittently will reinforce your training efforts.

THE *DROP IT* CUE

To teach your dog to drop something that he has in his mouth, he first needs to be reliable with *sit* and *stay* so that he doesn't run off with the object that you're using to

Hand signals paired with your verbal cues can reinforce the desired behaviors.

Food-training your dog is a great way to create a good bond. That bond gets your dog to respond to you and pay attention. That is why positive training works so much better, especially with more sensitive breeds.

—*Janice Dearth, AKC rally judge and provisional novice judge from Peyton, Colorado*

The words "Good" and "Yes" in training are used to shape and mark behaviors similar to the way that a clicker is used. Use "Good" to tell your dog that he's progressing toward the goal behavior and "Yes" to signify that he's completed the task and will now receive his reward. Your Boston will quickly learn what these words mean.

teach the *drop it*. Ask your dog to sit, and then give him something that he can't chew up quickly, such as a rawhide bone. As soon as the rawhide is secure in his mouth, hold a tasty treat over the dog's nose and issue the cue "Drop it." When your dog drops the rawhide to get the treat, say "Good" and reward him with the treat. Give the rawhide back to your dog and repeat this exercise three times. The last time you ask him to drop the item, give it back and walk away. This creates more cooperation, and he will learn to be more forgiving later when you ask him to drop something that you can't give back to him, such as your shoe.

THE *LEAVE IT* CUE

Once your Boston understands *leave it*, you will be able to keep him from putting forbidden items in his mouth.

One method to teach your dog the *leave it* cue is to get two treats and hold one in each hand. Hide one of the treats by closing one hand right away. Hold out your other hand to show your dog the other treat. Allow the dog to discover the treat in your open hand, but don't let him eat the treat. Instead, close your hand around the treat and say "Leave it." Don't move your hand or open up your fingers; just keep your closed hand held out in front of your dog. Allow him to lick at your hand, paw at your hand, or even nudge you to try to get you to give up the treat. Don't say anything to discourage these attempts. As soon as your dog stops trying to get the treat and turns away, immediately praise him and give him the treat that was concealed in your other hand. Continue to do this exercise over and over until your dog turns away as soon as you say "Leave it."

WALKING ON LEASH

Walking your dog has a multitude of advantages, including strengthening your bond, providing exercise, and expending some of your Boston's energy. However, walking an out-of-control dog is no fun for either of you. From the first time you introduce the leash, enforce good manners. Use a treat to lure the dog to your side and to keep him walking at your pace. If you're having trouble teaching your Boston good leash manners, consider taking a training class, which can help you train your dog to walk politely on leash amid distractions and around other dogs.

PHASING OUT TREATS

Anytime you train with treats, you'll eventually need to wean your dog off of them. The basic rule of using treats in training is that you use treats to reward the dog when you're teaching him something new, as the treats let him know when he's doing the task correctly. Once the dog understands how to respond to the given command, you can begin to decrease the frequency of the food rewards. With some dogs, you can eliminate treats altogether, but never hesitate to give the dog praise for a task well done. Boston Terriers love their owners' enthusiasm and praise.

Training Tips

- To help ensure repeated success, never call your dog to come to you for punishment.
- Keep all training positive. If you are becoming frustrated, end the session and wait until you feel that you have enough patience.
- Realize that your Boston can become frustrated, too. If your dog is making a lot of mistakes, take a break. Sometimes a short walk can refresh a dog if you are determined to do a bit more training.
- If you're having problems in your training with getting consistency from your dog, you may need to work on how you give cues. Try enrolling in an obedience or training class. This will not only help you learn how to train your Boston but also will offer him an opportunity for some socialization.
- Begin your training in an area where there are no distractions, such a quiet room in your house. Once your dog knows how to do a task, begin to add distractions, such as going outside. It is a good idea to practice the exercise until your dog learns to comply even amid distractions.
- Do not repeat a verbal command over and over; this will lessen the cue's effectiveness. If your dog doesn't respond to your cue the first time, make sure that you have the dog's attention before repeating it. If he doesn't respond the second time, try luring him with a treat to get him to perform the desired behavior.
- Keep lessons relatively short. A short lesson every few hours will be more effective than one long session per day.
- Realize that, when learning how to respond to cues, dogs need repetition and practice until the correct behavior becomes a habit.

Many times, owners can get away with poor training techniques and still manage to train their dogs. Likewise, many dogs can figure out what their owners want them to do even if their owners punish them for unwanted behaviors. Poor training techniques may be tolerated initially by your Boston Terrier, but they will not work well in the long run. Punishment is a negative way to manage unwanted behavior, and that negativity can become destructive in your relationship with your dog. We know that with sensitive Bostons, too much negativity can result in their displaying overly submissive behaviors, such as crouching and crawling as their owners approach or urinating submissively.

The real solution is to train for and reinforce the behaviors you want instead of punishing the behaviors you don't want. For example, as discussed in chapter 10, you can use the *leave it* cue to teach your Boston not to pick up your slippers (or any other object) and carry them to his bed to chew on. You do this by rewarding the behavior you want: as soon as your dog

Did You Know?

Although the breed's name has *terrier* in it, the Boston Terrier of today has lost most of his terrier-like desire for mayhem. Some males may still challenge other dogs if they feel that their territory is being invaded.

Consistency counts. If you find that your dog is not cooperating with you in your attempts to train him or modify his behaviors, make sure that you are giving clear and consistent cues. If you have a friend who knows something about training, have him or her watch you work with your dog to help determine where your communication has broken down.

turns away from those slippers, praise him and offer him something that he can chew on. By beginning with basic training, you develop a relationship with your dog in which he learns that he has to obey your cues. From the basic cues, you can work toward more complex training.

What you may find cute in a puppy can turn into a big, painful problem with an adult dog if not "nipped" in the bud.

NIPPING

Nipping problems most often arise in puppies. Nipping is a natural thing for a young dog to do as he explores his world with his mouth. Ideally, puppies learn not to nip from their littermates. Puppies, when playing with each other, begin to learn how to gauge if they're nipping too hard and how to use their teeth more gently. Puppies removed from the litter too soon, before eight to ten weeks of age, can fail to learn mouthing finesse. If you have a puppy with a nipping problem, you can do what his littermates would have done to discourage it. First, make a sharp, yip-like noise, as if you're in pain. If the puppy persists, increase the consequences by making the yipping noise and then turning away and ending the playtime or interaction with the young dog. Be aware that this process often needs to be repeated several times before the youngster realizes that his nipping results in no more attention from you. Be consistent.

WHINING

Whining is a natural behavior for a young puppy. It is how he expresses himself or gets attention from his mother. However, when whining or crying becomes a persistent habit, it becomes a problem for you. To solve the problem, you must first figure out why your dog is whining. Dogs will whine if they are uncomfortable; for example, if cold or in pain. Dogs will whine if they are bored

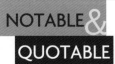

NOTABLE & QUOTABLE

Taking your dog to puppy classes or basic training classes helps fill your dog's training and socializing needs. This works to curb unwanted behaviors in your dog.
—Nancy Pappas, Boston Terrier owner from Security, Colorado

NAUGHTY DOG | **143**

Bostons can be vigorous chewers, so pay attention to what your dog is putting in his mouth.

or lonely. Some dogs will whine if they are overly excited and full of excess energy. However, seeking attention is one of the number-one reasons.

If your Boston is whining, first make sure that he doesn't need to go outside or that he isn't in pain or discomfort; in these cases, simply deal with the issue at hand. If your dog is whining because he wants attention from you, and you give him attention, you are rewarding the whining behavior. To discourage him from whining, reward him for being quiet. Don't say a word or make eye contact when he whines; stand quietly and turn your head slightly away from your Boston to emphasize that you are ignoring his behavior. If he persists in whining, pick up a treat and ask him to sit. When your Boston sits, he often will stop whining. Give the treat for the sit and, if your dog remains quiet, reward him with petting.

UNWANTED BARKING

A dog barks when he wants something or if he is excited. He will also bark if someone comes to the door. Your Boston will probably bark an initial "alarm" when someone comes to your house, which is fine, but then he needs to be quiet. There are a few ways to help encourage your dog to be quiet. One way is to take a few treats, give the verbal cue "Quiet," and give your dog a treat when he is quiet. Repeat the cue-and-treat process several times and in several sessions

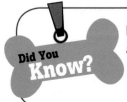

Did You Know?

Dogs, like people, have a teenage stage. In dogs, it begins at about five months and ends around one year. During this time, many dogs may be problematic, only to grow into much more charming adults. Employ patience during this stage.

during the day. With some practice, you'll be able to simply give the *quiet* cue when your dog is barking, and he will know what he has to do to get the treat.

BEGGING

Begging typically becomes a problem in dogs whose owners indulge them with treats from the table. It might start out with a morsel here and there, but soon the situation gets out of control. To prevent begging, never feed your Boston while you are eating. Instead, teach him to sit or lie down nearby until you are done. At that time, you can offer your dog a reward for his patience.

CHEWING

Chewing can be a big issue with Boston Terriers. A good way to deal with chewing is to give your dog something that he can chew safely. Chew toys marketed as indestructible may help satisfy your dog's chewing needs. Rawhides can be given as special treats but only under your supervision. You need to take a rawhide away from your dog when it becomes too small or if it starts breaking into smaller pieces that can be swallowed, posing a choking hazard or causing intestinal blockage.

Some dogs get into excessive chewing if they are not getting enough exercise. Set aside some time each day to take your Boston for a nice walk to relieve some of his extra energy. You can also engage your dog in play. Tossing a ball or flying disc for your Boston can not only entertain your dog but can also help burn off some energy that he might otherwise use for chewing. An added advantage is that the time spent with you, walking or playing together, helps your dog bond more strongly with you. That bond makes your dog all the more determined to please you by following your cues and behaving the way you want him to.

Prevent unwanted chewing through supervision and the provision of safe chew toys.

SMART TIP!

Use playtime as a reward for training. Although many dogs love food treats, many Boston Terriers love to play just as much. So don't just hand over a biscuit when your dog performs well; instead, toss a ball and play with him.

If you find that there are certain objects on which your Boston seems determined to chew, such as a cushion or a table leg, you can buy a chew-deterrent spray at a pet-supply store. These sprays don't discolor most items, but they do have a bitter taste, which discourages destructive chewing.

JUMPING UP

Smaller dogs, especially attention-loving dogs like Boston Terriers, often jump on people to get attention, as jumping up puts a dog closer to a person's face. One good technique to deal with jumping up is to countercondition your dog. As mentioned, when you use counterconditioning, you teach the animal to respond with a desired behavior instead of an undesired behavior in the presence of a certain stimulus. In the case of jumping up, your arrival is the stimulus for your Boston. To countercondition your dog, you will teach him to sit, instead of jump up, to get your attention. When your dog jumps on you, grab a treat and ask him to sit. When your dog sits, give him the treat to reward him for sitting, and then lavish him with the attention that he wanted in the first place. Pretty soon, your Boston will learn to automatically sit when he wants attention from you when you come home. Be sure to give your dog his treat for sitting, but don't forget to give him the ultimate reward of the attention he seeks.

Most dogs are opportunists when it comes to food—and Bostons are certainly no exception!

I've had some incidents with dog-to-dog aggression in Boston Terriers. It is really important to socialize them as early as possible, do structured training, and at the first signs of trouble, get professional help to [learn to] redirect aggression issues.
—*Nannette Nordenholt, dog trainer from Colorado Springs, Colorado*

FOOD STEALING

Dogs are opportunists by nature and will often make a grab for any unguarded food left anywhere that they can reach. One good way to teach your Boston not to steal food is to set up a training scenario in which you teach him when he can and when he can't have food. To do this, you need to first have taught the *leave it* cue from chapter 10. To begin training, set a piece of food on a table where your dog can reach it. A coffee table is usually well within the reach of a Boston Terrier. Attach your dog's leash and allow him to stroll up to the food on the coffee table. Just before he snatches the food away, say "Leave it." If your dog still goes for the food, use the leash to stop him. Wait until he turns his attention away from the food; when he does, praise him and give him a treat of higher value than the food on the coffee table. By "higher value," we mean something that your Boston really likes, not just his regular treats.

Repeat this exercise one or two more times, then quit for the day. Repeat the training scenario for several days in a row until your dog learns to walk away from any food sitting out on your coffee table.

DIGGING

Some breeds are more prone to digging, and some individuals are more avid diggers than others. Boredom often increases a dog's likelihood to dig, but there are other things that can trigger unwanted digging, such as a dog's trying to reach a dog on the other side of a fence. If your Boston is digging in an area where you don't want him to dig, put some of his feces in the hole he dug, and he should abandon digging in that area. The best course of action, though, is prevention, which means supervising your Boston's yard time and making sure that he gets plenty of activity and attention.

COPROPHAGIA

Coprophagia is the ingestion of feces. If your Boston is eating his stool, the first step is to try and determine why he is doing this. First on the list is to have your veterinarian analyze a stool sample to determine if your dog has a worm infestation. Internal parasites can suck nutrients out of your dog, driving him to eat his feces. You may also reevaluate your dog's diet or try adding a vitamin or mineral supplement to his food. A dog may start eating his feces out of plain boredom. If you are crating your dog too much, you need to restructure his routine so that he's getting enough playtime and companionship. Stress can also drive a dog to start this habit. If there is a lot of stress or tension in your household, it isn't unusual for a dog to react adversely. A dog may also become stressed if his owners use punishment and negative reinforcement in training. If your Boston Terrier is not getting enough positive attention from you or is experiencing stress, the solution is to change your relationship with your dog.

An owner whose dog is engaging in coprophagia may find that habit still persists even if he or she resolves the reason behind it. One solution is to keep your yard extremely clean. Another preventive is to add a product to your Boston's food that makes the feces taste bad to him. Check your petsupply store for such products. Some people have achieved the same result by adding crushed pineapple to their dogs' food.

AGGRESSION

Although many people think that dominance in a dog is the biggest reason behind aggression, fear is more often the driv-

ing factor. Some dogs resort to aggressive behavior to guard food or other possessions. With most forms of aggression, seeking professional help is recommended rather than trying to solve the problem yourself. Ask for recommendations for a behaviorist or trainer who employs canine behavior-modification techniques. Stay away from those who try to use force or harsh techniques. Retraining your dog is the real solution.

LEASH AGGRESSION

When on leash, some dogs strike out at other dogs who come near them. There are several reasons for leash aggression; for example, some dogs find that being restricted by a leash makes them feel territorial, while others act in an aggressive manner because they are afraid. If you have a Boston who acts aggressively when on leash, you need to do a little retraining.

One way to deal with your dog's lunging at the end of the leash is to reverse directions and walk the other way. Once your Boston settles down, ask him to sit and have him focus on you. When he does, reward him with a treat. You can keep your dog's attention on you until the other dog is far enough away that your dog no longer reacts. By doing this kind of training, you dog will soon realize that he doesn't need to lunge at another dog and that he should calm down and focus on you instead.

POSSESSIVE BEHAVIOR

Some dogs get protective of certain areas, including where they sleep. For example, if your Boston is lying on the couch or in your bed, he may growl if you try to move him. If you allow this kind of possessive behavior to continue, your dog may progress to biting.

One way to deal with this is to teach the *off* cue. Get several of your dog's favorite treats and go to the couch or other problem area. Pat that area and ask your Boston to jump up. As soon as your dog settles down, say "Off" and use one of the treats to lure to dog off of the area. Repeat this a few more times and then end the session.

Do several sessions like this over the next few days. Then, the next time you come across your dog sleeping in an area that he has been possessive of in the past, you can simply give him the *off* cue. Since you've already practiced this with him, he will most likely be willing to jump down when you tell him "Off." When he does, reward him with a treat and praise, then ask him to get on and off a few more times before you leave him alone to rest. Through this kind of training, many dogs will become less possessive about favorite areas because they have been trained to be cooperative about moving when asked.

SEXUAL BEHAVIOR

Males and females will sometimes mount other dogs or objects; some males will even mount people. A common misconception is that when one dog mounts another dog, it's a display of dominance, but some dogs do this just to have fun. To discourage this behavior, tell the dogs "No" and then physically separate them. If your dog is mounting you, tell him "No" and remove him. Block your dog's path so that he doesn't resume the activity. You may also want

If a Boston is refusing to obey a cue, you may need to switch from offering a reward to delivering consequences, but those consequences need not be punitive. For example, you can turn away from your dog when he jumps up so that you're not rewarding him with attention, but you don't have to yell at him.

to distract your dog with something else to do, perhaps by tossing a toy or offering something to chew. If your dog tries again to mount your leg, clap your hands loudly and use a firmer "No." If he still persists, put him outside or in another room for a few minutes for a short time-out.

LEASH PULLING

Even the most obedient Boston Terrier can be distracted by the world around him and pull on his leash when out on a walk. Letting your dog pull is not a good idea; aside from being impolite behavior, when done repeatedly, the pressure from the collar can damage his throat. If you have a dog who is very energetic on walks, and you haven't had much success teaching him how to walk politely on leash, then you need to consider using a device that will help discourage pulling.

Don't use a regular harness on your Boston; instead, try a head halter or martingale harness. If you want to use a head halter, you will have to look into those specifically designed for short-nosed breeds, as regular styles will not work with Boston Terriers or other brachycephalic dogs.

The martingale harness is a relatively new innovation. Unlike a regular harness, which still allows a dog to pull, a martingale harness is designed to prevent pulling. With this device, your dog's lead attaches at a point on his chest, and this works to redirect your dog toward you should he start pulling. Like a martingale collar, which gently tightens around a dog's neck, the martingale harness gently tightens around the chest and shoulders. This works well with many dogs, especially those who resist the head halter.

SEPARATION ANXIETY

A dog with separation anxiety typically engages in destructive behaviors when left alone in an attempt to relieve his anxiety. A dog may claw at the carpets, chew wooden moldings, scratch up furniture, or frantically paw at doors and windows. Many dogs who suffer from separation anxiety are by nature somewhat insecure. Unfortunately, many people do more to encourage separation anxiety than to help their dogs get over it.

If your Boston Terrier is suffering from separation anxiety, don't ever punish him for any destruction that you come home to. Punishment will only make your dog more upset about your departure and arrival, leading to a worse case of separation anxiety.

If you are in the habit of coddling your Boston, change the way that you interact with him. People who pick up, hold, and carry their dogs around all the time do nothing to help build their dogs' confidence. Insecurity can fuel separation anxiety. If you take your Boston somewhere, don't carry him. Unless your Boston is in a truly dangerous situation, let him learn to deal with the world around him with four paws on the ground. Playing with your Boston is another way to help him build up a feeling of security.

Modifying the way you leave and enter

the house can help your Boston. If you usually rush around in an anxious state before you bustle out the door, your dog can pick up on your tension, making him all the more anxious. Instead, allow yourself some extra time when preparing to leave the house. Give yourself an extra five minutes to sit calmly before leaving so that your dog can also calm down.

When you arrive home, don't greet your dog with a high-pitched, excited voice. If your dog acts excited and anxious when you come home, stand quietly and wait for him to settle down before you greet him. Emphasize a quiet and calm departure and arrival to encourage your dog to feel less anxious.

Another technique that may help your dog feel less anxious about your departure is to crate him in a quiet room before you leave the house. Be sure to give your dog something safe to chew on or a long-lasting treat to eat in the crate so he looks forward to going inside his crate and spending some quiet time there.

Doing things with your Boston Terrier can be fun for both of you. Some people prefer unstructured activities, such as throwing a ball in the backyard, while others like to explore their competitive side in dog shows or performance events. Since the Boston is a do-everything-with-you kind of breed, your dog has the potential to enjoy and succeed at a range of activities.

EVERYDAY FUN

Boston Terriers enjoy exercise, which has the added benefit of helping keep your dog fit and healthy. Since Boston Terriers need moderate exercise, it's a good idea to plan on doing some kind of activity with your dog every day. That activity can be as simple as taking a walk.

For people who are not used to walking, the concept of walking a mile can seem quite taxing. However, most people can walk a mile in twenty minutes, and a twenty-minute walk doesn't sound so bad. If you don't get a lot of exercise, having a Boston is a great reason to change your habits—both you and your dog will benefit. Begin by walking whatever distance is comfortable for you. The next day, go a

Did You Know? Volunteering to help at a dog show is a great way to learn about an event before you compete. Check with the local clubs in your area to find out if you can help.

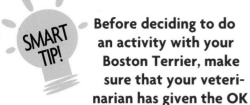

SMART TIP!

Before deciding to do an activity with your Boston Terrier, make sure that your veterinarian has given the OK for the type of physical exertion associated with that activity. Even if your dog doesn't have brachycephalic problems, you still have to be careful with your Boston in the heat.

little farther. Keep adding distance to your walk, and don't be surprised if after you reach a mile, you find that a second mile isn't that difficult. An added bonus to the physical fitness benefits for both you and your dog is that walking is mentally relaxing. So grab that leash and let your best pal enjoy some walking time with you.

If you have a fenced backyard with enough room for your Boston to run, allowing him outside can provide some activity, but most people overestimate the benefits of letting a dog loose in the yard. Sure, your dog will enjoy some time outdoors as a break from the house, but a yard doesn't offer a lot of entertainment—unless, of course, your dog takes up digging and running the fence with passing cars or pedestrians. So don't merely let your dog outside and expect him to get the exercise and mental stimulation he needs in a manner acceptable to you. Instead, use the backyard as a place to hang out with your dog. Your Boston will gladly keep you company while you do yard work, and he will enjoy playing with you if you toss a ball or other toy for him.

GOING PLACES AND DOING THINGS

Bostons can make great companions for people who enjoy hiking, backpacking, or other outdoor pursuits. If you go boating, get a life jacket for your Boston and bring him along. It isn't unusual for a Boston to want to ride with you in the car when you go out to do errands, but please make sure that you don't leave your dog in the car. Just a few minutes in the summer heat can bring a car to a potentially deadly temperature for your dog. Also be sure to use a doggy seat belt on your Boston when traveling in the car.

If you go on group dog walks or charity walks that allow dogs, take your Boston Terrier with you. Don't forget to put plastic bags in your pocket to pick up any droppings should your dog need to answer the call of nature on the walk. Your Boston will also enjoy any kind of activity in a dog-friendly park. You'll find that your Boston Terrier is eager to participate in events with you, hang out, and just plain have fun.

INDOOR ACTIVITY

Did you ever have one of those days when the weather is keeping you inside, but you feel like getting out and doing something? Your dog can feel the same way. And if you have kids, chaos can ensue. One cure-all for bored but antsy kids and Boston Terriers is to play a game of hide-and-seek.

To teach your dog this game, get a squeaky toy that he likes. Squeak the toy a few times and toss it for your Boston to get him interested in playing with it. Each time you toss the toy, say "Find it." When your dog grabs the toy, say "Good dog, good find it." Next, take a sheet or blanket and one kid. Grab a hold of your dog's collar and have the child take the toy and start squeaking it excitedly in front of your dog's nose. After a few squeaks, have the child duck under the blanket but keep squeaking the toy. Let go of your dog's collar and tell

him to "Find it." As soon as your dog gets to the blanket, have the child pull open the blanket and toss the toy for him.

Do this a few times and then stop for a while so your Boston stays interested in the game. If you play until he gets tired of the game, it won't be as exciting to him when you want to play again.

After your Boston learns that "Find it" means for him to look for the child with the squeaky toy, you can change the game. This time, take hold of your dog's collar and let your dog watch as the child goes around the corner with the squeaky toy. Have the child begin to squeak the toy and then tell your dog to "Find it" and let go of his collar. When your dog finds the child, have the child toss the toy and play with the dog for a few moments. The next time, have the kid go a little farther away before you have the dog find him or her. Again, only play a few times to make sure that you keep your Boston's interest.

The next time you play the game, do the same thing but with the child a little farther away than before. If your dog finds the child fairly quickly, have the kid try hiding in a closet to see if your dog can find him or her. Once your dog gets the hang of the game, you'll find that the child is enjoying trying to find new places to hide and the dog is enjoying going all over the house to find the kid. This keeps both child and dog occupied and entertained. Of course, you can play this game with several people who take turns hiding. And why not let your dog help you rediscover your more playful side? It can be great fun for all.

SHOWING AND COMPETING WITH YOUR BOSTON

Every year, New York City hosts the Westminster Kennel Club dog show, where top-quality dogs of all American Kennel Club breeds come together to compete. Although the focus of the Westminster show is conformation, there are many other types of events that can be fun to do with your Boston Terrier.

Conformation and Showmanship

The goal of conformation shows (known to most simply as "dog shows") is to determine which dogs conform most closely to their breed standards and are thus suitable for breeding. All-breed clubs and single-breed clubs host these kinds of shows.

In the conformation ring, a judge views each dog in a standing position and in motion. The judge gives each dog a hands-on evaluation to check that the dogs don't just look good but are indeed structurally sound and properly built for their breed.

Showmanship competition is offered at some conformation shows; these classes are especially popular for junior handlers, but some shows offer such classes for adults. In showmanship classes, the judge evaluates the handlers' style and technique in the ring rather than the quality of the dogs. For people who like to show their dogs but whose dogs don't compete well in the conformation ring, this may be a fun type of competition to enter.

it's a Fact

Dogs react to the tone and volume of our voices. By paying attention to how you give a verbal cue, you can more accurately communicate to your dog what you want him to do.

Obedience

Obedience trials in the United States trace back to the 1930s, when organized obedience training, developed to demonstrate how well dog and owner could work together, made its way across the Atlantic from England. Obedience trials are divided into different levels of difficulty, and a dog must earn a certain number of points for each exercise to achieve the title for the level at which he is competing.

At the subnovice and novice levels, dogs perform similar exercises, but some of the novice exercises are done off leash. Exercises include heeling, standing for an examination by the judge, and performing a *stay* in both *sit* and *down* positions. Open-level obedience requires a dog to heel off leash, sit when his handler stops, do a five-minute *down/stay* and *sit/stay*, retrieve a dumbbell over a jump, and do a broad jump on command. At the utility level, a dog must complete exercises that show his ability to discriminate scent and follow retrieving commands.

Rally

In more recent years, rally classes, which offer a twist on traditional obedience competition, have been offered. With the dog on the handler's left side, the dog-and-handler team moves through a rally course that consists of ten to twenty numbered signs. At each sign, the team stops to perform the indicated exercise and then move to the next sign. The exercises in rally are similar to many of those in obedience. Unlimited communication in the form

A nimble Boston maneuvers over the teeter during agility practice.

Most dogs do not reach physical maturity until they are around a year and a half old. For that reason, participation in more strenuous events needs to be delayed until the dog is officially done growing.

of commands and signals is encouraged between hander and dog, whereas in obedience, any extra cues are marked as faults. Scoring in rally is less rigorous than in traditional obedience. So if you want to train with your dog and compete in a less formal setting, rally may be a great way to have fun with your Boston Terrier.

Agility

Agility originated in the United Kingdom in 1977; AKC agility began in the United States in 1994. You no longer need an AKC-registered dog to participate in AKC agility, but the AKC is not the only group to offer this event. Two of the major agility organizations in the United States are the United States Dog Agility Association and the North American Dog Agility Council; both of these groups offer agility to all dogs, regardless of breed.

Agility is basically an obstacle course for dogs, requiring a handler to guide his or her dog over, through, and around obstacles such as jumps, ramps, tunnels, see-saws, and weave poles. Each run is timed, and different levels of competition offer different complexities in the course. Penalties are issued for going off course, taking too long on a course, or not completing an obstacle correctly.

There are two ways that dogs compete at agility trials. The first is against the other dogs participating in that particular show at that particular level. Placements are awarded to the dogs with the fastest times and the fewest course faults. The other way is for a dog to earn points toward mastering each level. The dog needs to complete the course within the allowed time and without course faults to earn a title at that level. The title awarded will depend on the organization putting on the event.

No matter what kind of agility you do with your dog, this event can be a lot of fun. The best way to get started is to enroll in an agility class in which you and your Boston Terrier will learn how to navigate the different obstacles and polish your communication and teamwork.

Flyball

Flyball is fun for dogs. It is a relay-type race that is open to all breeds and mixed breeds, not restricted by any particular registry. In this event, a team of four dogs compete against the clock. Dog teams are categorized according to height, with the shortest member of the team determining the height of the jumps. One at a time, the dogs run down the lane, jumping over a series of jumps on the way. At the end of the lane, a small box holds a ball. The dog hits a trigger board to release the ball, and once the dog retrieves the ball, he runs back to the starting point, at which point the next dog runs his leg of the relay. An online search can help you locate flyball clubs in your area if you are interested in joining a team or starting your own team.

Youth Competitions

Youth competitions can offer an opportunity for entire families to enjoy dog sports. The AKC, the United Kennel Club (UKC), and

From picnics in the park to a day of competition, your Boston will love being active with you.

many other clubs offer youth competitions. All of these clubs have a similar goal, which is to encourage young handlers to become involved in the world of dogs, whether in conformation showing or another type of sport, such as agility or obedience. For this reason, judging or scoring in youth competition puts as much, if not more, emphasis on the handler as on the dog.

Young competitors learn how to train their dogs and how to handle their dogs correctly. They learn the rules and procedures of competition, as well as what type of, if any, equipment to use. Competitors are expected to come prepared, to arrive on time, and to display a good attitude and sportsmanship. Proper and humane training methods are emphasized in all aspects of competition. Junior members are encouraged to seek help from experienced handlers, who are often willing to help younger participants.

Dancing with Your Dog— Canine Freestyle

In the world of dog sports, "dancing with your dog" is known as canine freestyle. Canine freestyle came into being in the 1990s; this modern sport is a creative interaction between dog and owner that mixes obedience, dancing, and tricks. There are two types of freestyle: heelwork to music and musical freestyle, both of which feature handlers and dogs performing to music. In heelwork, the focus is on the dog's ability to stay in variations of the heel position while his handler moves to music. In musical freestyle, the dog performs a variety of tricks and obedience skills with his handler, and there is a greater focus on the trainer's dancing ability and creativity.

If you are interested in either type of canine freestyle, you should align yourself with a freestyle organization. You'll find that the rules of competition vary from group to group and from country to country; however, most of the rules are based on a variety of technical and artistic merit points. Performances are done without training aids or leashes (except in some beginner categories). Competition categories include those for single dog-and-handler teams, pairs of dogs and handlers, and teams of three or more dogs and their handlers.

In heelwork competition, dog and handler remain close to each other at all times; there are no sendaways or distance work. In fact, the dog often appears almost invisibly tethered to his human partner as the team performs. Moves in heelwork routines include pivoting and moving diagonally, backward, forward, and back to front. This type of competition doesn't allow jumping, weaving, rolling, passing through the trainer's legs, and similar moves.

In the musical freestyle category, heelwork can be combined with distance work, sendaways, and more dramatic tricks such as jumps, spins, bows, rollovers, stationary dance moves, and other innovative actions. The dog is encouraged to play off of his partner's dance moves. It isn't unusual to see a smaller dog jumping into his handler's arms or over his or her back.

Dancing with your dog doesn't need to be competitive; it can be done just for fun. Simply put on some music and start to move. Encourage your dog to move with you by asking him to do a trick or two that he already enjoys doing. Bostons are good at picking up on your movements and your excitement, so keep your attitude chipper and give your dog lots of praise as you encourage him to follow along with you.

Disc Dog

Since most Boston Terriers are naturals at chasing flying discs, this sport is right up their alley. And like the Boston Terrier, disc-dog competition has its roots in the United States. Tossing a Frisbee went from a casual afternoon activity in a park to a nationwide competitive sport after one memorable incident.

On August 5, 1974, Alex Stein, a nineteen-year-old college student from Ohio, and his Whippet, Ashley, jumped over the fence and onto the field during a nationally televised baseball game. Stein began throwing Frisbees, and Ashley astonished the crowd with his disc-catching abilities as he raced and leaped high into the air. The announcers and the crowd seemed mesmerized by the unexpected entertainment, which lasted for eight minutes before Stein was escorted off the field and arrested. Those eight televised minutes fueled disc dog as a competitive sport.

In competition, the dog and owner form a team, and points are awarded to the team for catches at varying distances. Teams compete in divisions based on the skill and experience of the handlers. Some disc-dog competitions also feature freestyle events, which consist of short routines that are choreographed to music and can include the use of several discs. There are even long-distance events in which the longest catch wins.

Most competitions take place in the summer on flat, grassy fields, but there are

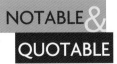

NOTABLE & QUOTABLE

I have a beautiful Boston named Delilah. Her energy level is on the ceiling, and she is going to make a great flyball dog!
—Jona Kalayjian, Boston Terrier breeder, dog-sport competitor, and 2 Fast 4 Paws flyball coach from Palm Springs, California

also winter contests held on soft snow. There are several organizations that run disc-dog tournaments. The Ashley Whippet Invitational, named after the dog who made disc-dog history, is a series of contests held around the world, culminating annually in a world-championship competition.

Boston Terriers tend to take to disc-catching naturally because they love chasing after and retrieving toys, and they love playing games. When you begin doing disc play with your Boston, throw the disc in a way that your dog can easily follow it through the air and catch it. Once a dog knows how to catch, he can learn the concept of running after the disc. After he's mastered this skill, you can begin to toss the disc higher to encourage your dog to jump and catch it. Start by tossing the disc just over your dog's head, and as your dog develops his skills, you can toss the disc higher and higher.

CANINE GOOD CITIZEN AWARD

The Canine Good Citizen (CGC) award is a noncompetitive event and is open to all dogs. Started in 1989, the program is designed to reward dogs who have good manners at home and in the community. This event is sponsored by the AKC, and all dogs who pass the ten-step test receive a certificate. Many countries have adopted similar programs to the CGC. Before testing for this award, you can enroll in a class to train your dog for the good manners and behaviors required for the certificate.

The CGC tests dogs on different types of training and interaction, including how they perform simple cues, how well they respond to their owners, and how they react to other dogs and to strangers. Since the CGC program rewards a dog's good manners and good behavior, many other programs—including many therapy-dog programs—require CGC certification as a prerequisite to therapy work. Although not all dogs pass the CGC test on the first try, working with your Boston on the CGC exercises will improve his general behavior.

THERAPY WORK

Therapy dogs are trained to provide affection and comfort to people. You'll find therapy dogs at work in hospitals, retirement homes, nursing homes, and schools, where they visit the patients and residents with their handlers. These dogs also work with people who are dealing with stressful or tragic situations, such as a disaster. Some therapy dogs visit people in hospice care; some are enlisted to help people with learning disabilities, speech problems, or emotional disorders; and some participate in library reading programs for children.

Therapy dogs must enjoy human contact and being petted and handled. A therapy dog's primary job is to allow unfamiliar people to make physical contact with him and show him affection. Many children and adults enjoy hugging animals or find comfort in simply petting dogs. A therapy dog needs to be tolerant to being picked up or to climbing up onto an individual's lap or bed. Some therapy-dog handlers have their dogs perform small tricks for their audiences or play carefully structured games.

The most important characteristic of a therapy dog is good temperament, something that's natural for most Boston Terriers. A good therapy dog must be friendly, patient, confident, at ease in all situations, and gentle. The benefits of a therapy dog's companionship include stress relief, lowered blood pressure, and improved spirits.

You'll find that your Boston Terrier is as adventurous as you are.

Therapy dogs are not service or assistance dogs. Service dogs have a legal right to accompany their owners in public places, while institutions may invite, limit, or prohibit visits from therapy dogs. Many institutions that allow therapy dogs have rigorous requirements, including testing and accreditation by a recognized therapy-dog organization. Most require your dog to have at least passed the CGC test, but further training and testing is typically required. Therapy-dog organizations and some dog clubs offer classes with specific training for therapy dogs. In this type of training, dogs are exposed to stimuli such as wheelchairs, medical equipment, loud noises, and elevator rides—things they are likely to encounter on therapy visits. Since these kinds of stimuli can initially unnerve some dogs, exposure and training can help them relax when in therapy environments.

NOTABLE & QUOTABLE

Although the American Kennel Club offers obedience, rally, conformation, and agility, there are other dog groups that offer agility, such as the USDAA and NADAC. Area clubs can be located through an Internet search. You can also search for flyball clubs in your area and attend an event to see if it's something that you and your dog want to do.

—Tia Reinschmidt, avid dog competitor from Parker, Colorado

Smart owners can find out more information about this bright and charming breed by contacting the following organizations. Members will be glad to help you dig deeper into the world of Bostons, and you won't even have to beg!

Academy of Veterinary Homeopathy: The AVH was founded in 1995, and its membership of veterinarians and veterinary students is devoted to furthering education and research in veterinary homeopathy. The organization also certifies veterinary homeopaths. www.theavh.org

American Animal Hospital Association: The AAHA accredits small animal hospitals throughout the United States and Canada. www.healthypet.com

American Dog Owners Association: The ADOA is a nationwide group of dog owners and fanciers who work together to further responsible ownership and owners' rights. www.adoa.org

American Holistic Veterinary Medical Association: This professional organization for holistic veterinarians promotes alternative healthcare techniques for the well-being of animals and supports research in the field. www.ahvma.org

American Humane Association: This nonprofit membership organization was founded in 1877 to protect children and animals. www.americanhumane.org

American Kennel Club: The AKC is America's oldest kennel club, established in 1884. Its website offers information and links to conformation, tracking, rally, obedience, and agility programs, registration information, member clubs, breed rescue, and more. www.akc.org

American Kennel Club Canine Health Foundation: This foundation is the largest nonprofit funder of exclusively canine research in the world. www.akcchf.org

American Society for the Prevention of Cruelty to Animals: The ASPCA was the first humane organization in North America. Its mission, as stated by Henry Bergh in 1866, is "to provide effective means for the prevention of cruelty to animals throughout the United States." www.aspca.org

American Veterinary Medical Association: This nonprofit association represents more than 80,000 veterinarians and is the accrediting body for American veterinary schools. www.avma.org

ASPCA Animal Poison Control Center: This resource, which is associated with the ASPCA, offers an informative website with lists of pet toxins and FAQs, as well as a hotline for animal poison-related emergencies that is available 24 hours a day, every day at 888-426-4435. A consultation fee may be charged. www.aspca.org/apcc

Association of American Feed Control Officials: The AAFCO develops and implements uniform and equitable laws, regulations, standards, and enforcement policies for regulating the manufacture, distribution, and sale of animal feeds, which results in safe, effective, and useful feeds. www.aafco.org

Association of Pet Dog Trainers: This professional organization for dog trainers was founded in 1993 with the goal of promoting continuing education and giving trainers a forum and a voice in the dog world at large. www.apdt.com

There are plenty of resources available to help you make a safe home for your Boston.

Boston Terrier Club of America: The BTCA is the AKC national parent club for the breed, devoted to the betterment and preservation of the "American gentleman." The club's website offers general breed information, event information, breeder referral contacts, rescue information, and more. www.bostonterrierclubofamerica.org

Canadian Kennel Club: Our northern neighbor's oldest kennel club is similar to the AKC in the States. www.ckc.ca

Canine Performance Events: This organization fosters fun and competition through agility trials. www.k9cpe.com

Delta Society: This organization offers animal assistance and therapy to people in need. www.deltasociety.org

Dog Scouts of America: This nonprofit hosts camps and educational programs for dogs and owners. www.dogscouts.com

My Boston has a sweet disposition and is always happy to see me. The simple things keep her happy. Basking in the sun, cuddling up in a warm blanket, a back scratch, or even a wet smooch are all things that keep her content. She offers me true companionship without asking for much in return. I can't imagine life without my Boston!

—Lauren Christiansen, Boston Terrier owner from Colorado Springs, Colorado

Before you take your dog to a dog park, visit the park and observe the dogs. If you see a lot of squabbles or large dogs roughhousing with smaller dogs, you may be wise not to take your Boston there.

Fédération Cynologique Internationale: This international canine organization includes eighty-four member countries and partners that issue their own pedigrees and train their own judges. www.fci.be

Love on a Leash: Share your dog's love with others through therapy work. www.loveonaleash.org

MidAmerica Boston Terrier Rescue: A nonprofit organization passionately dedicated to the Boston Terrier in an eleven-state area. The website is a wealth of information about adopting a rescue Boston, volunteering with the group, and breed-related topics. www.adoptaboston.com

National Association of Professional Pet Sitters: When you will be away from home, hire someone to watch and entertain your dog. www.petsitters.org

North American Dog Agility Council: This organization's website provides links to clubs, obedience trainers, and agility trainers in the United States and Canada. www.nadac.com

Pet Care Services Association: This nonprofit trade association includes nearly 3,000 pet-care service businesses in the United States and around the world. www.petcareservices.org

Pet Sitters International: The mission is to educate professional pet sitters and promote, support, and recognize excellence in pet sitting. If you need someone to watch your dog, start here. www.petsit.com

Therapy Dogs Inc.: Get your Boston Terrier involved in therapy work. www.therapydogs.com

Therapy Dogs International: Find more therapy-dog info at this organization's website. www.tdi-dog.org

United Kennel Club: Founded in 1898, the UKC is America's second oldest purebred dog registry and places an emphasis on performance events. www.ukcdogs.com

United States Dog Agility Association: The USDAA has information about agility training, clubs, and events in the United States, Canada, Mexico, and overseas. www.usdaa.com

World Canine Freestyle Organization: This organization proves that dancing with your dog can be a great idea! www.worldcaninefreestyle.org

TRAVELING WITH YOUR BOSTON

Car travel can frighten some dogs but exhilarate others. To help your Boston become acclimated to the car, start teaching him to be a good traveler at a young age. When you put your dog in the car, talk calmly to him; excitement can work against you. If the dog seems a bit apprehensive, take a moment to sit him on your lap and calm him down. Take your crate along in case you need to confine your dog until he learns to relax in the car. Some people always crate their dogs in the car; if you choose not to, then you will need to safely confine your dog with a special doggy safety belt. This device not only restrains the dog while in the car but also increases the dog's odds of surviving an auto accident, much like a person's seat belt does.

If taking a long trip with your Boston, buy a spill-proof travel water bowl so your dog can drink while on the road. Also bring a

Early socialization is the basis for all of the things that you and your Boston will do together and for making him welcome at dog parks, doggy day care, and the like.

stash of small plastic bags to clean up after the dog at potty stops. If you'll be staying overnight, be sure to make a reservation in advance at a hotel that allows dogs.

If planning air travel with your dog, the good news is that a smaller Boston Terrier may fit into a carry-on travel crate that you can stow under the seat of an airplane. The bad news is that some airlines do not allow brachycephalic breeds to travel in the cargo hold, so if your Boston doesn't fit into a travel crate of the approved size, you may not be able to fly with him. Either way, you must tell the airline in advance that you are traveling with a Boston Terrier.

If you are able to fly with your Boston, you will need to prepare him for the trip, starting a few weeks beforehand. To do this, put the dog inside the travel crate for ten minutes or so while you are in the same room with him; for example, while you are watching television. Give the dog

Buddy sleeps with us in our bed at night, and sometimes I'm awakened by loud snoring and snorting. I blame that on Buddy, too, although sometimes it is my husband, I'm sure.

—Martha Puckett, Boston owner from Monument, Colorado

something, such as a safe chew toy, to occupy him. Slowly increase the amount of time that the dog stays in the travel crate until he feels comfortable staying there with you nearby for a few hours. Having your Boston acclimated to his travel crate will make the airplane trip less stressful for the dog and for you.

BOARDING

If your Boston can't come with you when you travel, you must arrange adequate care for him while you're away. If you choose to board your dog, begin your search by asking other dog owners if they can recommend a good boarding kennel in your area. When you find one or more that you're interested in, arrange to visit and inspect each facility. Make sure that the dogs inside look clean and at ease. You don't want to leave your dog at a place where he is going to be stressed.

There are some boarding opportunities that offer care in a person's home. Some people will take on one or two dogs and care for them along with their own dogs. If you can locate this kind of a care situation, all the better for your Boston, who will enjoy the attention.

Whether you use a boarding kennel or a home-care setting, make sure that your dog is up to date on his shots, including a kennel-cough vaccine, which most boarding facilities require. Plan on booking your dog's stay well in advance, especially during busier times of year, such as during holidays, as better boarding kennels can fill up early.

PET SITTING

Rather than board their dogs, some people choose to have pet sitters come to their homes to attend to their dogs. This is especially economical if you have several pets or if you'd like other small daily tasks done, such as having plants watered or the mail brought in. Again, word of mouth is a good place to start your search—ask your dog-owning friends and your veterinarian for referrals. Some vet techs do pet sitting as a side job. The National Association of Professional Pet Sitters certifies pet sitters, and you can visit the website and search for a sitter at www.petsitters.org. This organization certifies professional individuals who are knowledgeable in canine behavior, nutrition, health, and safety.

MICROCHIPPING YOUR DOG

Identification tags can rub some dogs' fur and cause bare or raw spots, leaving some dog owners tempted not to attach the tags. Even owners who do put on tags find that the tags can detach and become lost. Although you can buy a collar with your dog's information embedded in it, and these collars are a great idea, a collar can also be lost. One of the best kinds of identification for a dog is a microchip—a small chip that contains the dog's name and an ID number that is registered to his owners—that is implanted under the dog's skin. This chip stays with the dog for his life. Your veterinarian should be able to implant a microchip for your dog. If your dog should become lost and cannot be identified by a collar or ID tag, the chip can be scanned by an animal rescue, humane society, animal shelter, or police department to access your information. Even if you are in a different state than your dog, you can be contacted and reunited with him. A good time to have a dog microchipped is when dog is spayed or neutered, although it is a relatively painless procedure that can be done at any time.

PUPPY KINDERGARTEN

Puppy kindergarten is a good way to introduce your dog to training and socialization. This type of class is typically open to dogs between the ages of three and six months. Be picky when choosing a class; get recommendations from other people and make sure that you enroll in a class that will teach both you and your dog the basics. Be sure that the trainer uses positive techniques. Also ask the trainer if the puppies are allowed to play together, and, if so, if the instructor takes any precautions so that more timid dogs aren't overwhelmed by more rambunctious dogs, or if the pups are grouped together for playtime according to personality.

Since puppy class is only once a week, you'll need to do things with your pup every day to keep the socialization going. You might take him to a pet-supply store that allows pets inside. You can also take your Boston to a park and allow people to interact with him. If you have a friend with a puppy, you can arrange puppy playtime.

DOGGY DAY CARE

Some people take their dogs to doggy day care once or twice a week, or even every weekday during working hours. This can help a dog burn off excess energy if his owners work full-time all week long, with the added benefit of interaction with other dogs and with people. Doggy day care can offer a variety of opportunities for your dog, including training, grooming, and even veterinary check-ups. Some facilities even offer webcams so that owners can check in and see their dogs throughout the day.

Before you enroll your dog in a doggy day care center, visit to look for:
• Escape-proof facilities with buffers so that dogs can't dash out an open door;
• Inoculation requirements for all dogs;
• Midday meals for young dogs;
• Positive, reward-based training (where training is available);
• Quiet areas where dogs can take breaks and naps;
• Aggression screening before dogs are accepted;
• Toys and playground equipment that is appropriately sized and safe for dogs of different sizes;
• Groupings of dogs that are similar in size and energy levels;
• An adequate number of trained supervisors to manage the dogs.

BOSTON TERRIER, a Smart Owner's Guide®
part of the Kennel Club Books® Interactive Series®

LIBRARY OF CONGRESS CATALOGING-IN-PUBLICATION DATA

Swager, Peggy O.
   Boston terrier / by Peggy Swager.
      p. cm. -- (A smart owner's guide)
   Includes bibliographical references and index.
   ISBN 978-1-59378-787-5 (alk. paper)
   1. Boston terrier. I. Title.
   SF429.B7S93 2011
   636.72--dc22

            2010046406

JOIN
Club Boston™
TODAY!